Brilliant common sense, from some...

– Rob Osborn, business co...

Really entertaining, informative and... would be, having read many of Andy's publications previously.

– Sarah Cotterill, global head of business continuity management, Computacenter

A great contribution to BCP realism... written by someone with a sense of reality of what actually goes on, and achieved with real insight and a touch of humour.

– Mark Mahoney, business continuity professional

Who'd have thought Practical Business Continuity 2 *would have been such a page-turner. Great job!*

– Nigel Mortimer, consultant, Trustmarque

A well written no nonsense practical guide full of tips to improve or build your own BCM capability. Andy makes complex concepts easy to understand and his considerable experience comes across as pragmatic and 'implementable'. I strongly recommend this book to all BCM practitioners.

– Rob Fletcher, head of ICT, GreenSquare Group

Andy Osborne's Practical Business Continuity Management 2 *provides 101 new tips which offer business continuity professionals of all types and levels of experience genuinely useful and helpful advice. Presented in a friendly and readable style, with a keen sense of humour, the tips are structured in such a way that readers can easily dip in and out, making this an essential everyday tool, not just a read and shelve resource. Andy has a knack for simplifying areas which may be perceived as complicated and his many years of experience shine through. Highly recommended reading.*

– David Honour, managing editor, Continuity Central

Practical Business Continuity Management

101 More Tips for *Effective, Real-World* Business Continuity Management

Andy Osborne

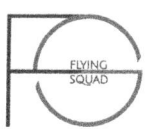

Practical Business Continuity Management 2
101 More Tips for Effective, Real-World
Business Continuity Management

ISBN 978-1-914209-00-0

eISBN 978-1-914209-01-7

Published in 2021 by Flying Squad Books

© Andy Osborne 2021

The right of Andy Osborne to be identified as the author of this work has been asserted by him in accordance with the Copyright, Designs and Patents Act 1988. A CIP record of this book is available from the British Library.

All rights reserved. No part of this book may be reproduced, stored in a retrieval system, or transmitted in any form or by any means, electronic, mechanical, photocopying, recording or otherwise, without the prior written permission of the copyright holder. No responsibility for loss occasioned to any person acting or refraining from action as a result of any material in this publication can be accepted by the author or publisher.

Contents

About the author	8
Foreword	9
Introduction	10

Chapter 1: Business Continuity Programme Management

Off to a good start	14
Going for gold	15
All the gear, no idea	16
One careful owner?	17
What's in a name?	18
Fun and games?	20
Re the business continuity plan	22
A business continuity capability vs a business continuity plan	24
A sense of direction	25
Movers and shakers	27
A standard approach?	28
Mind your language	29
An objective review	30
Let 'em have it?	31
Sticking it to them	33
Business continuity *mis*management	34

Chapter 2: Business Impact Analysis and Risk Assessment

The best of both worlds	38
The foresight saga	40
A healthy appetite	41
The devil's in the detail	42
The problem with probability	44
Two twos are four – but not always	45
It's likely that something unlikely will happen	46
Reality check	48
It's about time	49
Narrowing the focus	50
Fourth party risk	51
It depends	52
Four key questions	53
The downside of being a successful risk manager	54

Chapter 3: Business Continuity Strategy and Solutions

Mind the gap	58
Decision time	60
How normal is normal?	62
Perfuming the pig!	63
A business discontinuity plan	64
IT's not business continuity	65
Safety in numbers?	66
Don't blow your cover	67
Under cover?	68

Chapter 4: Incident Management and Business Continuity Plans

What's the use?	72
Make yourself a tome	73
A numbers game	75
A bag of spanners?	76
A reasonable assumption?	78
Keep it simple	80
A plan on a page	81
Idiot proof	82
The wheat from the chaff	83
The soft option – part 1	84
The soft option – part 2	85
A premium quality business continuity plan?	86

Chapter 5: Crisis/Incident Management

Crisis, what crisis?	90
Opportunity knocks	91
An issue with authority	92
A leading role	93
The magnificent seven	94
Tempus fugit	95
The deciding factor	96
Log it or lose it	98
What's the story?	99
Feel the rhythm	100
Questioning the answers	101
Fight, flight or film	102
A question of focus	103

Chapter 6: Crisis Communications

A matter of perception	106
The big issue	107
A hotline to your staff	108

The social club	109
Deal or no deal	111
No news is bad news	112
In search of the TRUTH	113
Making a statement?	114
The fear factor	115
Three-point turn	116
As easy as ABC	117
Who cares?	119
Breaking with tradition	120
'I MEAN' to say	122
A sense of rumour	123

Chapter 7: People Issues

Keeping one's own counsel	126
Personal effects	127
Self, self, self	128
Let's get personal	129
We're only human	130
One at a time	132
Personnel responsibility	133
A little knowledge can be dangerous	135
A personnel challenge?	137
Touchy feely	138

Chapter 8: Exercising and Testing

The proof of the pudding	142
A successful failure?	143
Ready for anything?	144
Imagine that	145
Keep fit	146
Warts and all	147
Are you sitting comfortably?	148
Testing the limits	150
Practice makes permanent	152
All in good time?	153
An exercise is an exercise is an exercise – isn't it?	154
A pair of debriefs	156

One final tip	158
Endnotes	159
References	160
Acknowledgements	161
Need some help?	162
Tip of the Month	164

About the author

Andy Osborne is a highly experienced business continuity, risk and crisis management consultant, trainer and author. In his 20+ years as an independent consultant, he has helped well in excess of 200 clients, of all shapes and sizes, worldwide and across a broad range of industry sectors, to develop, implement, prove and maintain their business continuity, risk and crisis management capability.

He is a firm believer that a) business continuity and crisis management is about developing a *capability*, not simply writing a plan and b) the role of a consultant or advisor is to simplify apparently complex processes and present them in a way that is easy to understand, not the other way around.

Andy is the author of several other books, including *Practical Business Continuity Management*, *Risk Management Simplified* and the intriguingly titled ebook *Ski Boots and Celery – A Compilation of Oz's Business Continuity Blogs*. His entertaining and amusing blogs, which link his day-to-day business and personal life experiences (often somewhat tenuously, as he is the first to admit) to business continuity, risk and crisis management themes can be read at www.acumen-bcp.co.uk/blog.

Andy lives in a semi-rural idyll near Evesham in Worcestershire (UK) with his long-suffering wife, two (allegedly) grown-up sons, one dog and assorted poultry. He is a keen gardener, beekeeper (although currently 'resting' in the absence of any bees) and an enthusiastic, though largely untalented cricketer, hockey player, skier, golfer, guitarist and juggler. When not indulging in these pastimes he runs his consultancy business, Acumen (www.acumen-bcp.co.uk) and does the odd bit of business continuity, risk and crisis management consulting!

To contact Andy or to book him for consultancy work, training courses or speaking engagements, email him at aosborne@acumen-bcp.co.uk.

You can also follow him on Twitter (@AndyatAcumen) and/or link to him on LinkedIn (http://uk.linkedin.com/in/andyosborneatacumen). He doesn't do Facebook, Instagram, Snapchat or Pinterest and is unlikely to start doing so anytime soon.

Foreword

I well remember Andy's original book, which I hugely enjoyed. I wondered if a new one could match the sharpness of his observations and his witty side-lines. No need to worry, this book is even better. Bang up to date with every tip showing he has been there and done it all.

In some ways, this book tells you all you really need to know about business continuity and why it doesn't always work as you might expect. My particular favourite is the people section and to paraphrase his quote 'machines are logical, people are emotional' – we all need to remember that every time we are perplexed that our elegant solution doesn't seem to work in practice.

Reading this book will probably tell you why. Better still, it will also help you not make the same mistake twice.

– Lyndon Bird, Business continuity management commentator, consultant and educator

Introduction

At long last, here is the keenly awaited follow-up to Andy Osborne's popular first book, *Practical Business Continuity Management*, which sold many copies worldwide.

It's the distillation of almost three decades of practical experience, helping clients of all shapes and sizes in pretty much every business sector, to develop their business continuity capability.

As with the previous volume, *Practical Business Continuity Management 2* won't tell you how to 'do' business continuity management. Like its predecessor, it doesn't bang on about life cycles, methodologies, processes or best practice guidelines and it certainly doesn't wax lyrical about standards or certification.

What it does do is present you with 101 practical tips, at least some of which are almost certain to help you develop and enhance your organisation's business continuity *capability*, helping to ensure its robustness and fitness for purpose.

The tips are grouped into relevant chapters, occasionally somewhat arbitrarily, as arguably some of the tips would sit quite happily in more than one chapter. Each chapter relates to one piece of the business continuity 'jigsaw'.

However, as with *Practical Business Continuity Management*, this is not really a book that's meant to be read from start to finish. Rather, the reader is encouraged to dip in and out as the need or fancy takes them.

POWER TIP Specific parts of certain tips have been highlighted with the icon shown here to emphasise a particularly key point – one that, in the author's opinion, is something really important that the reader should take particular note of. In most cases this opinion has been confirmed by feedback from a number of business continuity practitioners, including (though by no means limited to) those who were kind enough to review and comment on the book's various drafts (see page 161), one of whom referred to several of the highlighted elements as 'power tips'.

Wherever you are on your particular business continuity journey, you should be able to find tips that will give you some food for thought, if not the proverbial 'light bulb moment'. To this end, the 'Follow-up actions' pages at the end of each chapter are there for you to make a note of any tips in that chapter which struck a chord, along with any actions you intend to take as a result.

So, save yourself a decade or three, have a read and feel free to use any of the tips, as presented or modified to fit your particular situation, to enhance your organisation's business continuity *capability.*

Chapter 1
Business Continuity Programme Management

No matter how good the team or how efficient the methodology, if we're not solving the right problem, the project fails.

> – William W. 'Woody' Williams

Off to a good start

A full-blown business continuity programme can be a daunting thing, particularly for someone who's new to the subject. There's just so much to get to grips with – agreeing a policy, business impact analysis, risk assessment, strategy development, plan production, testing, awareness-raising and so on. And each of these areas has a whole host of activities associated with it. So where on earth to start?

The thing is, a business continuity implementation project, let alone the ongoing programme, can take an awfully long time from initiation to having the strategy and plans fully in place and tested (if, indeed, they ever are). But if some sort of business disruption or crisis happens in the meantime, there will be a whole load of 'stuff' to deal with, whether your strategy and plans are in place or not.

POWER TIP

So an effective incident management capability is absolutely essential. And rather than waiting until halfway through the project before thinking about it, why not sort out your incident management team right at the outset? Decide who should be in it, brief them on their roles and responsibilities and get them up to speed by way of an incident management exercise.

This needn't take forever. But by doing it, even if the analysis, strategy and detailed plans aren't complete, you'll have a fighting chance if the 'stuff' should hit the fan in the meantime.

Going for gold?

It's amazing how many organisations, as their first foray into business continuity management, launch into the programme all gung-ho, with a view to implementing an all-singing, all-dancing, gold-plated, best-of-breed ISO (or other applicable standard) certifiable business continuity management system – and all within ridiculously ambitious timescales. Less surprising is the number that spectacularly fail to meet that goal.

While the aspiration may be laudable, the truth is that for most organisations it's just not realistic.

Because as often as not, the people who will have to do the work aren't as excited at the prospect as those asking for it. Possibly because they don't really know what business continuity management is or what it entails. Probably because they have plenty to do already and the thought of 'yet another initiative' doesn't thrill them, resulting in an unwillingness or inability to commit the necessary resources. Perhaps because of a culture that doesn't embrace the level of formality required. Or an 'it'll never happen to us' mentality. Or because there's no real support from senior management, despite the lip service.

If any of these apply in your organisation, rather than aiming for a gold-plated approach and failing, it's almost certainly better to start off by aiming for something a bit more realistic and achievable. Like a basic capability, based on some pragmatic analysis, and some simple plans, along with an exercise or two, rather than a huge amount of complexity and a correspondingly huge amount of effort. Something that allows people to 'get it', that they're more likely to embrace than push back against. Something that advances the cause, gets the momentum going and that can be built upon going forward.

Gold-plated might sound very nice, and may be necessary in certain situations, but sometimes a good, solid, cast-iron foundation is much more useful and appropriate.

All the gear, no idea

There's a certain breed of sportsman that's instantly recognisable. Although it occurs in other sports, the phenomenon is most prevalent in golf, and any serious golfer will have observed it on numerous occasions.

This type of golfer has all the latest, most expensive equipment so they really look the part. Until, that is, they get onto the first tee, whereupon they scuff their drive or lash it sideways into the trees, water, rough or adjacent fairway – or miss the ball completely. Because, while they might have all the flashy gear, they have little or no golfing ability. And no amount of whizzy kit or equipment is going to improve their game, because the basics just aren't there.

A similar thing can sometimes be observed in the world of business continuity management. Before doing anything else, a misguided individual buys the whizziest looking, most expensive tools they can find, in the misguided belief that this is all that's required to implement a robust, fit-for-purpose business continuity capability. They mistakenly think that these tools will miraculously do everything for them. But because they don't really have the knowledge or ability to use them properly, and because they haven't done the groundwork first, they're often disappointed with the results.

While there are undoubtedly some excellent tools available that can assist an organisation to improve its business continuity capability, those tools on their own won't magically provide that capability if it's not there in the first place. There's usually a bit more to it than that. Ask any proper golfer.

One careful owner?

All too often, some 'lucky' person is given the task of implementing a business continuity plan for their organisation only to find out later that, unbeknown to them, someone already had a go two or three years ago and there's an out-of-date plan languishing in someone's office. Amazingly, it sometimes turns out that this is the third or fourth attempt, but that no one seemed to know about the previous efforts. Why is this?

The answer can often be summed up in one word – 'ownership'. The task of producing a business continuity plan was given to someone as a project, which they duly did, ticked the box and moved on. But no one ever took ownership of said plan and, as a result, it never got looked at again, let alone updated or tested. The end result is a complete waste of time and effort, and little or no benefit to the organisation in terms of its resilience.

If business continuity management is to be successful, ownership is essential. And not only ownership in terms of one person having overall responsibility, but ownership in terms of people seeing it as something important that they play an active part in maintaining, exercising and testing.

To be truly successful, business continuity management has to move on from the initial project to become an ongoing process; something that's seen as part of people's normal jobs, rather than something that someone else in the organisation does.

So what would you rather have: an effective plan that's kept up to date, that people know about and that has a fighting chance of actually working, or something that's left to gather dust and results in a huge amount of effort in reinventing the wheel every few years?

What's in a name?

In case you haven't heard yet, the latest buzzword in business continuity circles is 'resilience'.

And, as is so often the case when a new term or concept appears, no one seems to be able to agree on what resilience means.

Is it just the business continuity industry looking to re-package itself or is it something completely different? Is it just the same old business continuity stuff with a new name, or is it something much bigger that happens to include business continuity management as one of its elements? Is resilience a part of business continuity management or is it the other way round? Is it just a way of getting the attention of senior people who have steadfastly refused to take an interest in business continuity management thus far? Or is it merely an excuse for unscrupulous consultants to sell something that looks and sounds a bit different, or for institutions to launch yet more standards, along with the associated documents and audit fees?

Almost certainly it's all of these things, depending on who you are and who you talk to. Let's face it, the business continuity world can't even agree on a common glossary of terms, an issue it's been debating for decades now, so what chance is there of gaining a common agreement on what resilience means anytime soon?

And does it matter anyway, as long as we're all working towards the common goal of making our organisations more resilient? Which probably includes elements of business continuity, IT continuity, risk management, supply chain resilience, compliance, information security, physical security, cyber security, crisis management and whatever else the organisation in question wants to include under the resilience banner.

As with many of the buzzwords, acronyms and terminology before it, the debate over what resilience means is set to rumble on for some time yet. In fact it's likely that there will never be complete agreement from all interested parties. So in the meantime, perhaps those of us involved in the debate should refrain from spending too much time debating and focus on what we can do to make our organisations a bit more resilient. Whatever that means.

Fun and games?

Incredible as it may seem to your average, dyed-in-the wool business continuity professional, the fact is that the majority of 'normal' business people don't find the subject of business continuity management particularly enthralling.

Why is this? There are, after all, some elements of the business continuity process that are, at the very least, vaguely interesting and, in some cases, actually quite challenging or thought provoking.

One reason may be the way that it's usually packaged. How often do we see the person leading the process begin by a) spouting doom and gloom about all the terrible things that might befall our organisation and b) spending hours describing the business continuity life cycle? You know the one: this life cycle is usually illustrated by a diagram comprising a circle surrounded by words like analysis, strategy, plans, testing, maintenance and so forth. And many a seasoned business continuity professional has been known to rattle on about this process for hours on end.

Then there's the business impact analysis, usually the first activity (other than sitting through the aforementioned presentation) that the business people are asked to participate in. Unfortunately, most business impact analyses are about as exciting as watching paint dry. And when you consider that most people have an awful lot of other things vying for their time and attention, is it really any wonder that they don't fully engage with a programme that starts like this?

But it doesn't have to be like that. While the various elements of the business continuity life cycle have to be addressed in some form if the resulting capability is going to be worth anything, they don't have to be approached in a way that makes people switch off from the outset.

There are a number of things that can be done to make the business continuity programme more interesting and engaging. Examples include:

➤ ***Starting with an exercise rather than a business impact analysis. And maybe using a format for the exercise that's entertaining or light hearted, rather than doom laden and pressurised. It might, for instance, include an element of competition, or the event might be structured like a game or a quiz show, rather than yet another meeting or navel-gazing session.***

POWER TIP

➤ Using such games and competitions throughout the programme to stimulate discussions about important issues. You might, for instance, pit teams against each other and award points or prizes for the winners or those who correctly identify whatever it is that you want them to.

➤ Engaging with the creative people in your marketing team to come up with some interesting, thought-provoking awareness materials or to create a 'brand' for the programme.

There's no law that says business continuity management has to be dull – it just happens that way in many organisations. While the above suggestions won't necessarily result in a laugh-a-minute romp that people shun their other day-to-day activities to participate in (and, let's face it, what other business activities *are* like that?), it might make them more inclined to get involved.

So why not give it a go in your organisation? All it requires is a bit of creativity. And, yes, there may be a bit more effort involved in the planning and preparation, but if you can engage people that effort will be repaid many times over in results compared with the more typical, same-old-same-old, dull-as-dishwater business continuity approach.

Re the business continuity plan

It's often said that 'change is the only constant in business', and there any number of events that may initiate significant change. Mergers, acquisitions or disposals, changes in business strategy, major projects, development of new products or services or entering new markets, to name a few, often bring reorganisations, restructures and various other re's to contend with.

In the midst of all this turmoil, it can be all too easy to take our eye off the business continuity ball, perhaps because there are other things clamouring for our attention or because resources are stretched more than ever before.

And does it really matter anyway if the names and contact numbers in the business continuity plan haven't been updated for a while?

Well maybe not; maybe we'll still be able to muddle through. But there may be other changes that, if they're not reflected in the business continuity strategy and plans, could seriously reduce our business continuity capability.

For instance:

➤ If the organisational structure has changed, does the business continuity structure still fit or does it need redesigning?

➤ If there have been changes to the business model, or to the key products and services, or to the activities that underpin them, does our previous view of what was most critical still hold true or do we need to revise our assessment?

➤ Are the underlying business continuity strategies and the solutions that support them still applicable or should we revisit them?

➤ Are the recovery time and recovery point objectives on which those strategies and solutions were based still valid or do they need to be reassessed?

- ➤ If key people move (either within or out of the business), do their business continuity roles and responsibilities need to be reassigned, and are the people that they're reassigned to up to the job?
- ➤ Do our training or awareness requirements need to be re-evaluated?
- ➤ Have our risks changed and are there, as a result, any holes in our mitigation measures that need to be repaired or reinforced?

While a business continuity plan that's slightly out of date may not be the end of the world, a business continuity strategy that's no longer relevant and a reduced capability or redundant solutions are a different matter entirely.

After (or better still, when preparing for) any major business change, why not **re**solve to **re**view, **re**assess and **re**vise (along with any other re's you can think of) your business continuity arrangements, particularly in light of any **re**organisations or **re**structures, to make sure your business continuity capability isn't **re**duced as a **re**sult?

A business continuity capability vs a business continuity plan

Many organisations focus on producing 'the plan' as the main aim of their business continuity programme. But, sadly, the plan itself won't save the business in the event of a major disruptive incident.

What *will* save the business is key people making key decisions and taking key actions – the business continuity plan merely supports that process. It's important, but a business continuity *capability* is far more important.

Developing a business continuity capability requires a number of things, including:

POWER TIP

➤ *An effective strategy that meets the needs of the business, plus realistic and workable solutions to deliver that strategy.*

➤ *Proving the strategy, solutions and plans, by exercising, testing and rehearsal, and by challenging and validating assumptions. This includes proving the incident management, communication, technical recovery and business recovery capability.*

➤ *Awareness, education and training. Key players need to know their roles and responsibilities and may well need some education and training to help them be effective in their roles.*

A business continuity *capability* doesn't come about through merely writing a plan then putting it on a shelf to gather dust – there's a teeny bit more to it than that.

So which would you rather have? And more to the point, which do you actually have?

A sense of direction

Despite the fact that any project managers reading this are likely to throw up their hands in horror, we all know that a large proportion of significant projects don't actually run to timescales or within their original budgets. And this is certainly true in the case of many a business continuity project. So why is this? Well, one reason could be that often the business continuity project isn't treated as a 'proper' project, so it's not given the focus it deserves.

A proper project needs several things. It needs some terms of reference; it needs to be managed and planned; it needs resourcing; it needs senior-level sponsorship, support and direction; and it needs progress to be reported to those affected by it.

Much of this can be achieved by setting up a business continuity steering group. A steering group will give the business continuity efforts a higher profile, enable those implementing the strategy, solutions and plans to understand senior management's requirements, help senior management to understand the issues involved and ensure that all interested parties are kept up to speed with progress.

So who should be on the steering group? Well, it needs to be people with some clout. And all key parts of the business should be represented. There are no hard and fast rules and membership will differ from organisation to organisation, but you might want to consider the following:

➤ business continuity project sponsor

➤ business continuity manager/project manager

➤ operations director/chief operating officer

➤ IT director/chief information officer

➤ information security manager

➤ director(s)/senior manager(s) from the most critical business functions

- internal auditor
- risk manager
- human resources director/manager
- finance director/manager
- facilities manager.

POWER TIP *So if you don't already have a business continuity steering group, then why not consider setting one up? It could just give your business continuity project the focus and sense of direction it's been crying out for.*

Movers and shakers

Your auditors (and, if you have one, your audit committee) can be powerful allies in your quest for an effective business continuity management programme. Aside from instilling fear and despair in those within the organisation who have something to hide, they have an envious ability to shake things up and get things moving. In short, they are effective activity creators.

But you need to get organised if you're going to use them to best effect. Rather than trying to elicit their help on an ad hoc basis, it's much more effective to get hold of their audit schedule in advance so you know who they'll be talking to, about what and when. Then you can highlight, in advance, any outstanding business continuity issues that need to be followed up (such as actions from previous exercises and tests, plan reviews and updates, and so forth) and give the auditors time to build the relevant questions into their forthcoming audits.

So if, despite your best efforts, your business continuity management programme is suffering from a bit of inertia, why not have a friendly chat with your auditors and see if you can get them to shake things up and create a bit of activity for you? **POWER TIP**

A standard approach?

Many organisations aspire to certification to a recognised business continuity management standard, such as ISO 22301[1], AS/NZS 5050[2], NFPA 1600[3] or any one of a number of related standards.

And why not? After all, gaining certification to a standard is guaranteed to result in a robust, fit-for-purpose business continuity strategy and plan isn't it? The problem is, in reality, it's not!

Granted, relevant standards can provide a sound framework showing all the widely accepted, best-practice steps in the business continuity management process, which is a very good thing. And following the guidelines in the standard or its associated guidance document *should* give you a fighting chance of ending up with a half-decent business continuity management system (or BCMS – as if we needed yet another abbreviation!). But it's not a *guarantee* of an effective BCMS – or, more importantly, of a business continuity *capability*.

Certification merely confirms that you followed the process to the satisfaction of an auditor (who, incidentally, might not actually be a business continuity expert themselves), which is all well and good. But in the same way that you could probably achieve certification to a quality standard by producing naff doughnuts or concrete life-jackets, as long as you always produce exactly the same naff doughnuts or concrete life-jackets in exactly the same way, merely following a process doesn't guarantee that the end result will be any good.

The bottom line is that it depends how you apply the process to your situation. A robust business continuity capability requires a tad more than doing the minimum required to get a tick in a box from an auditor.

So by all means use one of the recognised standards as the benchmark for your business continuity programme. And by all means go for certification if that's what floats your boat. But just take a step back and think *why* you're doing it – to get a tick in that particular box, or to actually make your organisation more resilient?

Mind your language

It's fair to say that business continuity practitioners inhabit a slightly different world to most 'normal' business people. It's a world of threats and impacts and recovery objectives; of incidents and interruptions, crises and disasters; of backups and restores and contingencies and workarounds; of recovery strategies and teams and plans. And when someone lives somewhere for any length of time, it's only natural to pick up some of the local lingo. Which is all well and good when we're talking to other locals who understand it.

But there can be a tendency to assume that the rest of the world speaks the same language. And the fact is that many 'normal' business people don't get particularly excited by 'business continuity speak'. So a better approach might be to avoid it altogether and use language and terminology that the whole business actually understands.

For instance, if the audience isn't excited by words like 'business impact' or 'recovery time objective', why not simply talk about what's critical to the success of their part of the business, what they depend upon to deliver it and how long they could be without it before it really started to hurt? If business continuity doesn't particularly float their boat you could try not using those two words in the same sentence – or at all for that matter. And as they probably have more than enough acronyms, abbreviations and buzzwords of their own to keep them amused (or confused), they might actually appreciate not hearing any of ours.

At the end of the day, it's far more important that the people on the receiving end of our attention understand what we're on about and buy in to it than us being precious about our industry jargon, no matter how much *we* might like to use it.

An objective review

It's important to keep our business continuity plans up to date. That almost goes without saying. But what exactly do we mean by keeping our plans up to date?

Most organisations with a business continuity plan will assign someone to review it periodically – in particular, to check that the names and contact details of the various team members are kept up to date. Which is an important activity. But there's a bit more to it than that.

There are essentially two reasons for reviewing and updating our plans.

First, to ensure the plans' content – the names, contact details, checklists, etc. – remains current.

Second, and just as importantly, to ensure that the strategies and solutions that underpin the plans remain fit for purpose and continue to enable us to meet our continuity objectives. Which implies that now and again we need to review those objectives and the strategies and solutions that support them.

Many organisations focus entirely on the operational detail of the plans and neglect the strategic elements. If that sounds familiar, you might consider adding a periodic strategic review to your plan maintenance programme. Otherwise, while you might be able to contact people without too much difficulty, it may well be to tell them that the plan doesn't work!

Let 'em have it?

You've probably noticed that the general level of business continuity awareness has grown in recent times – which is good news. But it probably means that your customers, prospects, business partners, investors or other stakeholders are increasingly taking an interest in *your* business continuity arrangements. In fact, if you haven't been asked about them yet, it's probably only a matter of time.

It's highly likely that at some point you'll be asked by someone for a copy of your business continuity plan. But should you send it to them or not?

Well actually, in most cases it's not necessary. And in any case, the detail of your plan is largely nothing to do with them! Think about it – your plan probably contains personal or confidential information, such as names, addresses and contact numbers, commercial details or other sensitive stuff.

It's almost certain that you wouldn't just send a copy of your business or marketing plan or your budget forecast or your employee database or details of how you run your business to a third party, just because they asked for it. So why should the content of your business continuity plan be any different?

POWER TIP

Rather than sending a copy of your plan, a better approach might be to send a summary of what you've done and what you're doing, for instance that:

➤ you've appointed a business continuity manager or co-ordinator

➤ there's a senior-level steering group in place

➤ you've done a business impact analysis to identify the time-critical activities and their recovery time objectives

➤ the key risks to the continuity of your business have been considered and appropriate steps taken to mitigate them

- ➤ you've implemented a strategy and appropriate solutions to meet the identified recovery requirements
- ➤ there's an incident management and business continuity framework in place, the relevant teams have been established and team members briefed on their roles and responsibilities
- ➤ incident management and business recovery plans have been documented
- ➤ there's an ongoing programme of exercising and testing
- ➤ the strategy, solutions and plans are regularly reviewed and updated
- ➤ the business continuity management system is in line with a recognised standard, such as ISO 22301[1], AS/NZS 5050[2] or NFPA 1600[3], depending on where you are in the world.

The vast majority – particularly if they actually know anything about business continuity management – will be more than happy with this approach. In fact, there's a fair chance that they'll be much happier than if you just send them a copy of the plan.

Of course, if you haven't actually done any of the above, you'll probably get found out, whether you send a copy of the plan or not!

Sticking it to them

Many organisations, quite rightly, recognise the importance of education and awareness in their business continuity programmes. Indeed, some spend significant amounts of time, money and other resources on awareness-raising activities. Sadly, though, all too often these efforts fail to gain people's interest, let alone embed any level of awareness. So why is it that so many business continuity awareness programmes are ineffective? The answer is often twofold.

First, at the risk of offending large numbers of business continuity practitioners and consultants, the sad fact is that quite a lot of business continuity training or awareness sessions just aren't very interesting. At least not to the audience that they're being delivered to. While business continuity principles and life cycles and standards, and the myriad acronyms and abbreviations (see 'Mind your language', p.27) that are constantly bandied about, may be interesting to someone whose working life revolves around them, the reality is that most of those who live outside the business continuity ecosystem just aren't that turned on by them.

Second, there's a thing called the 'forgetting curve'. This, depending on your preference and level of cynicism, is a mathematical formula, a psychological phenomenon or a statement of the blooming obvious, the gist of which is that over time we forget things we've learned if we don't do something to make them stick. Therefore, while a one-off presentation or an exercise or tabletop walkthrough every year or two might get you a tick in the audit or compliance box, it will do little if anything to reduce the steepness of said forgetting curve.

So, remembering that most people don't live and breathe business continuity and taking into account the forgetting curve, those of us involved in awareness-raising should a) do our utmost to make our sessions a little more interesting and relatable (to our audiences, that is, not to our fellow business continuity geeks) and b) find ways to regularly remind people, preferably through the practical application of what they've learned, so that at least some of it sticks.

Business continuity *mis*management

There are lots of things you can do to improve your chances of developing a robust and fit-for-purpose business continuity capability. Listed below are seven ways to make sure it's a spectacular failure!

1. Leap straight into the plan-writing phase without any thought for analysis, strategy or the specific solutions that will underpin the plan

2. Take a pre-written business continuity plan template and simply insert your organisation's name. Don't bother to customise it any more than that – no one will notice

3. Do it in isolation. After all, there's no need to trouble anyone else when they're all so busy with far more important things than thinking about the survival of the business. In particular, don't bother to get any executive support for the business continuity programme

4. Think of as many different scenarios as you possibly can and write a separate plan for each. Ideally the resulting document will be about three feet thick!

5. Implement an IT recovery plan without talking to the business about what they *actually* need

6. Don't bother to exercise or test. Everything's bound to just work perfectly without any problems or glitches

7. Don't provide any training, awareness or education for those who have roles within the plan. After all, they'll just know instinctively what to do and how to do it when the time comes

The above list will seem utterly ridiculous to the more enlightened reader, but they are all things that have been tried by real people in real organisations with predictable results. For goodness' sake please don't join them.

Follow-up actions

This page is for you to note any tips from this chapter that struck a chord, along with the follow-up actions you intend to take to benefit your business continuity management programme in your organisation.

TIP/PAGE...	TO MAKE THIS TIP WORK FOR ME I WILL...

Chapter 2
Business Impact Analysis and Risk Assessment

Analysis is the critical starting point of strategic thinking.

> – KENICHI OHMAE, *The Mind of the Strategist: The Art of Japanese Business* (1982)

The best of both worlds

There are several ways to carry out a business impact analysis, from simply sending out questionnaires, to carrying out one-to-one interviews, to holding group sessions or workshops. And there are pros and cons to each of them. For instance:

- The questionnaire-only approach is less time consuming for the person carrying out the analysis, and a large number of people can potentially be 'hit' simultaneously. But there's a significant trade-off in terms of the accuracy of the data coming back and the ability to validate it.

- The one-to-one interview approach (often with a questionnaire involved) gives the opportunity to question and to better understand the responses, although it's still possible for the interviewee to misrepresent their own importance, and it can be time consuming for the interviewer.

- The workshop approach has the advantages of getting people involved and of sanity checking the data by peer review at the point that it's given, so it's much more likely to be accurate. But it can be difficult to schedule and there's a risk that some people might switch off when the focus isn't on their area of responsibility.

A business impact analysis often comprises two distinct elements – first, identifying the impacts of a disruption, which, in turn, helps to identify the recovery time objectives; and second, identifying the specific requirements for recovery (people, facilities, IT and other technology, plant, equipment, etc.) in order to meet those objectives.

One suggestion, therefore, is to use a combination of the workshop approach *and* the one-to-one interview approach. That is, hold a senior management workshop to discuss and assess, as a group, the business impacts and recovery time objectives, then follow it up with a series of shorter, one-to-one interviews with business function representatives to identify detailed recovery requirements. In this way you get the best of both worlds – immediate validation of the key information needed to develop the business continuity strategy and the ability to go into as much detail as you need to with each business area.

Whatever you do, don't just send out some questionnaires and expect to get sufficiently accurate information back to be able to determine a meaningful business continuity strategy. It's good to talk!

The foresight saga

Hindsight, as they say, is a wonderful thing. It allows us to be wise after the event. With the benefit of hindsight it's much easier to see something that now seems obvious. How often have you heard the words 'it was an accident waiting to happen' *after* the accident has happened?

Effective risk management aims to make us wise *before* the event – to use foresight, rather than hindsight, to identify potential problems and prevent the accident, incident or disruption from occurring in the first place. And horizon scanning – keeping an eye on the news and events in other parts of the country or overseas – can help to highlight emerging trends, open our eyes to potential risks or give us a head start on developing situations that may affect us.

Hindsight may be wonderful in the saying, but in reality it's a bit pointless. So don't neglect the risk management and horizon scanning elements of your business continuity management programme. If you can develop a culture of foresight rather than hindsight, it will make your organisation more resilient and it might just mean that you never have to use your business recovery plans in anger.

A healthy appetite

Everyone has their own personal appetite for risk. Some people think nothing of taking huge risks, both in their business and personal lives, while others are far more reserved, to the point of being almost totally risk averse. Most of us fall somewhere in between.

Similarly, all organisations have a 'corporate' risk appetite, which dictates the types and levels of risk that the organisation, or at least the senior management team that directs it, is willing to take or to accept. The problem is that it can be very difficult to pin them down and get them to define the corporate risk appetite, partly because it's actually quite difficult to put into words. As a result, few organisations bother to do so, and fewer still actually document and publish a formal statement of risk appetite to their managers and staff, which can make life a bit difficult for them in terms of their risk management efforts.

But if our risk management programmes are to be effective, we really need those at the helm to give us a clue as to the levels of risk that they're willing to accept and those that they aren't. For instance, a high level of strategic or equipment risk may be acceptable, whereas the opposite may well be true of health and safety or reputational risk – so one approach may be to ask for clarification of the acceptable levels of risk in each of the various categories.

Another approach might be to ask, after the most significant risks have been identified and quantified via a risk assessment, what you consider to be the most significant risks, for confirmation of those that they're willing to accept and those that they want to address in some way. Ideally get this confirmation in writing as this always helps to focus the mind!

Whatever approach is taken, getting a steer from those at the top can be hugely beneficial. It helps get their buy-in, ensures a consistent approach, makes the risk assessment process more productive and can potentially save a significant amount of wasted time and effort by preventing managers and staff from barking up the proverbial wrong tree.

The devil's in the detail

While there's more than one way to conduct a business impact analysis (see 'The best of both worlds' on page 38), a fairly typical approach is to identify the organisation's key activities and to assess the impacts of disruption to each of them over a series of predetermined time periods. Different types of impact, both financial impacts (such as lost revenue, impact on share price, fines or other penalties, additional costs, etc.) and non-financial impacts (such as health and safety/welfare issues, reputational impacts, regulatory issues, etc.) are usually considered.

The process often goes something like this:

1. Starting with the first activity on the list, assess the various applicable financial impacts of disruption to the activity for each of the predetermined time periods. This typically covers a time span ranging from a few minutes or hours to a few weeks, so there are likely to be half a dozen or more time periods.

2. Repeat activity number one, this time assessing the applicable non-financial impacts of disruption to the activity.

3. Repeat the process for every activity on the list.

4. Derive the recovery time objective for each activity from the (probably rather large) table of assessed impacts. This is usually done by determining the point at which the impacts hit a predetermined 'intolerable' level and setting the recovery time objective at a point before the intolerable level is reached.

The main reason for using the above approach is that we've always done it that way – or, at least, quite a lot of people in the business continuity 'industry' have done it that way for quite a long time. That and the fact that this approach has found its way into standards such as ISO 22301 – largely because the main contributors to those standards are those who have done it this way for quite a long time. And, on the subject of a long time, as you can probably imagine (or remember, if you've ever been through the process), this approach can take a serious amount of time.

The main purpose of a business impact analysis is to confirm the recovery time objectives for the activities that support the provision of an organisation's key products and services, and to provide some justification in terms of the impacts that would be felt if those activities were disrupted. But does that really mean we have to go into *so* much detail when considering those impacts?

POWER TIP

A more pragmatic and less time-consuming approach, particularly if you don't aspire to certification to a specific standard, is to come at it from a slightly different angle, starting with an assessment of an activity's recovery time objective and then considering the impacts if that recovery time objective isn't met, rather than the other way around. The end result is usually spookily similar – provided, of course, that the right people are involved.

This less detailed approach won't suit everyone, and you may well have good reasons for using what is, after all, a tried and tested process. But 'because we've always done it that way' isn't necessarily a good reason for continuing to do it that way, when another way might be perfectly adequate for your needs.

The problem with probability

A typical risk assessment process involves the identification of potential risks, which are then quantified and rated, based on the likelihood of the risk occurring and the impact if it does.

Sometimes other terms, such as 'probability', 'frequency', 'consequences' or 'severity' are used in place of likelihood and impact. To a large extent, it doesn't really matter which you use – whichever you feel more comfortable with.

You might just bear in mind, however, that the word 'probability' can suggest a mathematical or scientific exactness that may not actually exist, which may be a good reason to avoid it.

In truth, risk management isn't an exact science and, while those obsessed with statistics might argue otherwise, the 'probability' of many unexpected events is largely unknown.

This doesn't mean, however, that we shouldn't give it some thought. Probably!

Two twos are four – but not always

It's fairly common practice in risk assessments to use a numerical scale when estimating likelihood and impact. A one-to-four scale is often used, with one being the lowest and four the highest. The likelihood and impact 'scores' are usually multiplied to give an overall risk rating, which is then plotted on a risk matrix – essentially a graph with likelihood on one axis and impact on the other. This is a perfectly reasonable way of quantifying and prioritising risks, which is more than adequate for the risk assessment needs of many organisations.

However, this approach comes with a health warning. It's important to realise that the numbers are really only there for convenience, and a level four likelihood isn't necessarily (in fact it almost certainly isn't) four times as likely as a level one or twice as likely as a level two. Similarly, a level four impact isn't four times as bad as a level one, or twice as bad as a level two. Indeed, the increase in likelihood or impact between level one and level four could well be twenty- or fifty- or a hundredfold or more (exponential).

The important thing here is where a risk falls on the matrix, as this will help us to consider which risks we ought to do something about and what we ought to do to mitigate them. A high-likelihood or high-impact risk needs to be considered, whatever the overall 'score' that arises from some overly simplistic, arbitrary 'calculation'. And if a risk sits anywhere in the top right-hand corner (high likelihood *and* high impact), action needs to be taken, full stop, regardless of any pseudo-scientific or quasi-mathematical scoring system that was used to determine its placement.

It's likely that something unlikely will happen

Most business continuity life cycle diagrams include risk management or risk assessment somewhere in the process.

For many this means one or more risk assessment workshops, whereby a number of risks are identified and rated, based on the likelihood of each risk occurring and the impact if it does (see 'Two twos are four – but not always' on the previous page). This is a tried, tested and commonly used approach in a number of risk management applications, from health and safety to operational risk, so it's often used for assessing business continuity risks too.

The problem with this approach in a business continuity context is that the risks identified are, more often than not, of the low-likelihood, high-impact variety. So, whatever rating system is used (the most popular being to multiply the likelihood and impact 'scores'), the overall rating for the vast majority of the identified business continuity risks usually comes out as low; or, at best (or worst, depending on which way you look at it), medium. Which means that, in the risk register, they're colour-coded as green or amber and seldom, if ever, is any meaningful action taken to mitigate any of them. Which, in turn, means the exercise was, in all probability, largely a waste of time. While this may seem a cynical observation, unfortunately it's a depressingly common scenario.

But importantly, while each individual risk may have a low likelihood of occurring, taken collectively there's potentially a much higher likelihood that *something*, at some point, is going to go wrong. As Aristotle once said, 'Είναι πιθανό ότι τα πράγματα μάλλον απίθανο να συμβεί θα πρέπει να' (at least according to Google!). Or to put it another way, 'It is likely that unlikely things should happen'. And he was right. Unfortunately, though, it's nigh on impossible to predict with any certainty what that something might be or when it might happen.

So, while there may be a few obvious risks that we probably should consider (provided, of course, that we're actually going to do something to mitigate them), rather than spending a huge amount of time brainstorming oodles of different low-likelihood, high-impact risks that no one thinks will happen anyway, a more productive use of management time and brain power might be to put more emphasis on identifying the *impacts* of losing our key assets, whatever the reason.

Because the good news is that if we get our business continuity strategies and solutions right, while we might not be able to prevent everything that could possibly go wrong, the resulting contingency plans should mitigate a large proportion of those low-likelihood, high-impact risks that would otherwise languish undisturbed in the depths of our risk registers.

Reality check

One of the typical outputs from a business impact analysis is a list of recovery time objectives for the infrastructure, systems and services – workspace, IT systems, plant, equipment, telephony, etc. – that support the organisation's key activities. This information is extremely useful, if not essential, to those determining the business continuity strategy and the solutions that underpin it.

But there's an important and all-too-commonly experienced issue to watch out for. It involves our old friends *communication* and *assumption*.

As often as not there will be gaps between the identified and the currently achievable recovery time objectives. This in itself isn't the problem. The issue comes when those gaps aren't communicated back to the business. Because, in the absence of any information to the contrary, their assumption is likely to be that they'll get what they asked for during the business impact analysis. And incorrect assumptions lead to invalid plans and a lack of continuity capability.

The solution is simple. All it requires is that we close the loop and communicate the reality back to those who contributed to the business impact analysis. While they may not like what they hear, it will at least allow them to plan their contingencies, manual workarounds or other mitigation measures, based on assumptions that are realistic. And, therefore, to develop plans that stand a chance of actually working.

It's about time

The term 'recovery time objective' has been around for so long now that you'd think that there would be a pretty-much universal understanding of what it means. This isn't always the case, however. There's one area in particular where there's often a huge gulf in that understanding, and that's the issue of recovery time objectives for IT systems.

Business people will typically, and quite reasonably, assume that the recovery time objective for an IT system starts at the point of disruption, as does the recovery time objective for a business activity.

IT people, on the other hand, will usually, and just as reasonably, assume that the recovery time objective starts at the point when the decision to invoke the IT recovery plan is made. Because, in fairness, how can they possibly commit to meeting a recovery time objective that includes an unknown, and possibly lengthy, decision-making process that's often completely out of their control? Clearly they can't. But that's exactly the situation that many IT departments find themselves in.

POWER TIP

The answer is actually quite straightforward. It boils down to communication and awareness. All of the interested parties need to understand what's involved in meeting a recovery time objective – the whole process, not just the technical recovery part – and the timescales involved in each part of that process, including the decision-making element.

This understanding may even help to reduce the recovery time, as the decision-makers might be motivated to make the invocation decision a bit quicker if they fully understand the consequences of delay. If not, at least the IT people shouldn't have to unfairly take the flak when a recovery time objective is exceeded through no fault of their own.

Narrowing the focus

Anyone who's ever been involved in a risk assessment workshop will know that once you get started you can identify a shed-load of risks. There are just so many of them out there.

But while some risks are potentially extremely serious, there are many others that are somewhat less significant. And, let's face it, it's the significant risks that we need to focus on. So we need to sort the wheat from the chaff and avoid getting too bogged down in stuff that isn't overly important.

One way to do this is to focus the risk assessment on our essential or time-critical functions, processes or assets and to set a specific objective for the workshop, such as identifying risks to cash flow or to the supply chain or to the continued operation of a critical process, facility or piece of equipment.

There is, of course, therefore the implication that we know what's essential or time critical. And, if we haven't already done so, an excellent way of identifying these things is to do a business impact analysis – *before* doing the risk assessment. But that's another story.

Fourth party risk

More and more these days, organisations are thinking about supply chain continuity and their dependence on third party suppliers. Which is an eminently sensible thing to do. After all, if we have critical suppliers, whose failure or non-performance would cause us significant problems, it makes sense to ask them some pertinent questions about their risk management and business continuity capability.

But how many of us consider the 'fourth party' suppliers – in other words, our key suppliers' key suppliers – or even understand who they are?

There are numerous examples of organisations being at significant risk because they are reliant on a third party supplier, who in turn relies on a third party supplier of their own – particularly when this 'fourth party' supplier turns out to be the proverbial 'Fred in his shed', with no continuity capability at all.

While it's clearly a good idea to ask our key suppliers about their business continuity arrangements, we might want to consider, if we haven't done so already, asking them what consideration they've given to their own key suppliers' continuity capability. And, depending on just how critical they are to us, maybe even that of their suppliers' suppliers too.

The further we can drill down and understand the key dependencies in our supply chains, the better we can understand and mitigate our supply chain risks. After all, a chain is only as strong as its weakest link.

It depends

Traditional risk management techniques usually revolve around creating a list of all the bad things that might happen, ranking them in some way according to likelihood and impact and adding a corresponding list of mitigation measures, many of which never actually get implemented. While this approach often provides the required tick in the box for an auditor, as often as not all that we're left with is a risk register and a feeling that we're missing the point slightly.

The trouble is that for all but the most obvious ones, anticipating specific threats is often a bit hit and miss and largely a matter of guesswork. And the process of assessing likelihood and impact is usually no more scientific that holding a wet finger in the air. In any case, we can almost guarantee that the problem that ultimately hits us won't be one of the risks we previously identified. And it'll probably be something that's outside of our control anyway.

So is there a better way?

One way might be to stop worrying so much about the specifics of what might go wrong, particularly if it's something that we have no control over, to focus instead on what we need to go right and identify what we depend upon for that to happen. By looking closely at the dependencies within a process, activity, system, business, environment, project, piece of machinery or whatever, we can determine where failure could prevent our success and identify appropriate contingencies.

Mapping our dependencies can help us to identify vulnerabilities that need to be addressed and secure ourselves against unknown threats, whatever they are and no matter how difficult they are to predict. And if our boat's still floated by the traditional risk assessment process, dependency modelling can help us to be far more targeted than the typical 'scatter-gun' approach.

If nothing else, focusing on the positives, rather than the negatives might make risk management slightly less depressing for those involved!

Four key questions

Some people think business continuity management is complicated. But when you get rid of the arcane terminology, life cycle diagrams and the plethora of abbreviations, acronyms and jargon that business continuity practitioners typically love to bandy about, it's really quite straightforward.

It's about answering four very simple but very important questions:

1. **What** is important to the organisation in meeting its commitments and strategic objectives?

2. **Why** are these things important, in terms of the impacts that would be felt if they were unavailable?

3. **When** do our critical activities and their supporting infrastructure need to be available, in order to avoid unacceptable impacts?

4. **How** do we ensure they are available when they're needed?

The first three questions will be answered by a bit of analysis, in particular the business impact analysis. The fourth is addressed by the development and implementation of the business continuity strategy, solutions and plans (more of which in chapters 3 and 4).

How complicated does that sound?

The downside of being a successful risk manager

The trouble with managing risks successfully is that the benefits often go unnoticed. When things go horribly wrong it can be very visible, sometimes quite dramatic, sometimes quite distressing. But when we avoid things going wrong people are generally none the wiser. And people generally don't give much thought to the risk that never materialises.

Consider the example of a production manager in a manufacturing company who recognises the risk of a hazardous chemical spill. He carries out a risk assessment and concludes that, owing to current working practices, there is a high risk of a spill occurring, the consequences of which would be extremely serious. So he convinces the board that processes need to be tightened and staff need to be trained. The board finally agrees, although they aren't particularly happy about the cost. Rigorous new procedures are implemented, resulting in complaints from staff who thought the old ways were fine and who are unhappy that the new processes take more time and effort. A programme of training is carried out, which team leaders complain about because it takes staff away from day-to-day operations for a short time. Pretty much all the production manager gets for his trouble is grief. But, as a result of his actions, the chemical spill doesn't occur, no one dies, the factory isn't closed down by the Health and Safety Executive, the reputation of the company remains intact, the workforce still have jobs and none of the board members are prosecuted or sued.

You'd think the production manager would be hailed as a hero, but sadly in real life that just doesn't happen.

So if being a hero is your aim, forget about managing your risks – you'd be better off letting things go horribly wrong so that you can demonstrate your heroism in the face of adversity! Or you could just take the quiet satisfaction of knowing that, because of your efforts, no one had to be a hero after all.

Follow-up actions

This page is for you to note any tips from this chapter that struck a chord, along with the follow-up actions you intend to take to benefit your business continuity management programme in your organisation.

TIP/PAGE...	TO MAKE THIS TIP WORK FOR ME I WILL...

Chapter 3
Business Continuity Strategy and Solutions

I believe that people make their own luck by great preparation and good strategy.

– Jack Canfield

Mind the gap

Several of the tips in this book make reference to the need to validate the assumptions associated with our business continuity strategies and plans. Examples include 'A reasonable assumption?' (page 78), 'Personal effects' (page 127) and 'A personnel challenge?' (page 137).

But it's not only invalid assumptions that result in gaps in our business continuity capability. Sometimes our chosen strategies just don't meet the needs of the business; or they fail to consider important elements.

For instance:

➤ Have you thought about technology other than IT – for instance telephony, manufacturing or test equipment?

➤ On the people front, does your strategy address the unavailability of key personnel?

➤ Have you considered how the loss of a critical supplier or a disruption in the supply chain might affect your ability to provide your key products or services?

➤ Does your premises recovery strategy actually give you the capability to accommodate the necessary people and equipment, and carry out the activities that your analysis says you need, within the timescales that have been identified and agreed?

This list is by no means exhaustive and the specifics will vary from organisation to organisation. The point is that the strategy, and the solutions that underpin it, probably needs to address a wider range of issues than just IT or office recovery. Does yours?

Here's a suggestion – one that's perhaps not for the faint hearted: why not add to the front of your business continuity plan, preferably in big, bold, highlighted letters, something along the lines of 'gaps in the strategy' or 'risks not addressed'? That way everyone will know that there are gaps that haven't been plugged and no one will be under any illusion as to what the strategy actually provides. And, just as importantly, what it doesn't.

Decision time

'It's about time' (page 49) discussed a common difference of opinion, between the folks in IT and those in the business, as to what constitutes a recovery time objective for an IT system. It suggested that both parties need to understand what's involved, from a *process*, rather than a technical point of view, in meeting an IT recovery time objective, and the associated times needed to carry out each part of the process.

Because if we know how long it takes to recover a system (and we should, because we've tested it, haven't we?), and we know how long it takes to make the environment available, deliver media or equipment, relocate people to the recovery site, or whatever else we need to do (all of which we've also tested, haven't we?), we can work backwards from our recovery time objective and know exactly how long we have to make the decision to invoke our plans.

As an example, let's assume we have a recovery time objective of 12 hours for a particular IT system. And let's assume that the recovery strategy involves restoring the operating system, the application and its data onto equipment at another location, from our offsite backups. Because we've tested (haven't we?), we know it takes two hours for our technical boffins to travel to the recovery site, an hour to configure the hardware and a further six hours to restore the operating system, application and data. In total, that's nine hours, from the time that the proverbial button is pushed and the boffins are given the go-ahead. So, we now know that we have a maximum of three hours from the point of failure to make the decision to invoke. And if we don't decide within three hours we can't possibly meet our 12-hour recovery time objective. Full stop. No ifs or buts.

This basic, but important, bit of understanding is a great help to both the decision-makers and the IT people. It helps the decision-makers because they now know exactly how long they have to make their decision. In the above example, they only have three hours. But they do have three hours, so they can take a little time, if necessary, to make a reasoned decision. And it helps the IT people because if the decision-makers can't decide within three hours, it's them, not the IT folks, who get to carry the can if the recovery time objective isn't then met.

How normal is normal?

When putting together our business continuity strategies, solutions and plans, a common assumption is that the ultimate objective is to return to normal following a major disruption. But what do we mean by 'normal'? More often than not, we mean recreating the status quo.

But some disruptive incidents are so significant that returning to normal may not be feasible or even desirable. Moreover, the disruption or 'disaster' may even provide an opportunity to do things differently.

For instance, we might choose to:

➤ relocate a facility rather than rebuild it in its current location

➤ outsource an activity that's currently done in-house

➤ re-engineer processes that are less efficient than they could be

➤ discontinue a less profitable product or service.

The point is that, if we're not careful, we can waste an inordinate amount of time and effort planning for something that wouldn't actually happen in reality.

So rather than just taking the path of least resistance and assuming the objective is to get 'back to normal', perhaps we should consider what a 'new normality' might look like.

Clearly this will be up to the strategic decision-makers, so it's a good idea to talk to them and get their take on things. There is, of course, a possibility that they might not want us to know what they're thinking, or at least not make it common knowledge. In which case, we might just have to resign ourselves to some time-wasting after all.

Perfuming the pig!

Anyone can write a business continuity plan. In fact that's the easy bit. And it's very easy to make the business continuity plan look very convincing. Names and contact details, a few checklists and a bit of blurb at the start about how seriously we take business continuity within our organisation can work wonders.

But it's also very easy to write a business continuity plan with no substance to it. One that essentially says 'we'll get a few key people together at the time and make it up as we go along'! There are any number of plans in existence that basically say this.

But what about the underpinning strategy and solutions? What's in place to ensure that we can actually meet our objectives in the event that we have to invoke our plans for real?

The plan is one thing but the strategy and solutions (not to mention the testing and exercising and awareness and education and ongoing review and maintenance) that turn a plan into a *capability* are quite another.

You can make the plan look as pretty as you like, but if the underlying strategy and solutions or assumptions are flawed it's just a cosmetic exercise.

As a former colleague of the author, an experienced business continuity practitioner with an interesting turn of phrase, was fond of saying, 'It doesn't matter how much perfume you put on a pig, at the end of the day it's still a pig!'

A business discontinuity plan

When considering our business continuity strategies and plans, it's quite usual to think about the different options for ensuring the continuation of various activities.

But in some cases, a strategy of *discontinuity* (i.e. deliberately deciding to suspend an activity for a period of time – or even to cease it permanently, rather than trying to keep it going), might be appropriate. Examples might include cases where:

- the cost of implementing a continuity strategy is prohibitive or significantly outweighs the benefits
- an existing legacy process wouldn't be done in the same way if it were set up now
- there's an unprofitable or low-profit activity that we carry on doing because we always have
- we have insufficient resources to continue or recover all of our key activities in the short term
- the 'disaster' gives us an opportunity to change what we do and/or the way we do things.

Clearly the decision to discontinue an activity, whether for a specific period or permanently, is a strategic one that needs to be made by appropriately senior people. And it's a good idea to assess the impacts and risks prior to taking that decision. But a deliberate strategy of business *dis*continuity isn't necessarily as off the wall as it might at first appear.

IT's not business continuity

Back in the mists of time, in almost all of the organisations that were doing any sort of business continuity (or, in those days, 'disaster recovery', which sounds far more exciting!), it was being done by the IT department.

Over the years, as the discipline has evolved – from disaster recovery planning, through business continuity planning, to business continuity management – the focus has broadened from being solely IT-related. In some cases, that is – but by no means all.

Even in these enlightened times, it's surprising, and somewhat worrying, that there are still plenty of organisations where business continuity management is seen as being purely to do with IT recovery; or where only the IT people are taking it anything like seriously.

But what's the point of recovering your IT systems if you don't have anywhere for your critical people to go? or if the manufacturing plant isn't operational? or if your customers or other stakeholders can't contact you? or if your supply chain isn't there anymore? or if the press or your competitors are having a field day at your expense? or if your cash flow has stopped flowing?

The reality is that, while IT is an extremely important element of almost all business continuity strategies and plans, it isn't the only element – not by a long chalk.

To be really effective, business continuity management needs to have an organisation-wide focus. It needs to consider *everything* that's important to the continuity of critical business activities (the clue's in the name after all!). And yes, that almost certainly includes IT, but if you think that IT's the only thing that's important to your organisation you're almost certainly missing the point.

Safety in numbers?

As a key element of their crisis management capability, many organisations utilise mass notification tools, which provide the ability to send text, email and other types of messages to large numbers of people simultaneously. Which is a very useful thing to be able to do.

Some of these tools have additional bells and whistles, such as the ability for recipients to respond with an 'I'm safe' message at the touch of a button and a handy dashboard of responses. Which also sounds like a great idea.

It does, however, beg the question: what, exactly, are you going to do with the responses?

For instance, if 85% of your staff reply to say they're safe, does that mean that 15% aren't? Not necessarily. There's a whole host of reasons why they might not respond – their phone may be switched off; they might be in a meeting and ignore it; there might not be a mobile signal where they are; or maybe they just can't be bothered. All you can really be sure of is that they haven't replied.

And for those who have replied to say that they're safe, does that guarantee that it'll still be the case in five minutes, or 15 minutes, or an hour? No, all you can really be sure of is that they felt that they were safe at the time they responded. Which, depending on the situation, doesn't necessarily mean you can forget about them, as they may still be at risk.

So, while at first sight the ability to quickly elicit an 'I'm safe' response seems really useful, unless you have a strategy and associated processes in place to deal with the responses, it may not be as helpful as you first thought.

The point is that, as with any solutions, technological or otherwise, we need to think through how we're going to use them, and the potential implications, *before* we rush into implementing them, if we're to reap the expected benefits.

Don't blow your cover

The subject of insurance often comes up when considering our risk management and business continuity strategies and plans – partly because insurance can be an important mitigation measure and partly because there may be significant implications at the time of a 'disaster' or major incident that need to be considered and, therefore, planned for.

It's one thing to understand what's covered by our various policies (which, it has to be said, many of us don't), and quite another to understand the mechanics of the post-incident claims process. For instance, there may be certain actions in your business continuity plan that require approval from your insurers before you can carry them out – like sourcing new premises or plant or equipment. Failure to understand how the process works could have serious financial implications or significantly delay recovery, or both.

One thing to consider is that the insurers will almost certainly appoint a loss adjuster. Indeed, the loss adjuster may well be one of the first people on the scene after the emergency services. It's as well to bear in mind who they're working for – and that isn't you! There's a big clue in the name: loss *adjuster*. Their primary objective is to 'adjust', i.e. *reduce* your claim; to minimise the insurer's losses. And, because that's their raison d'être, they tend to be pretty good at it.

So you could do a lot worse than to appoint your own loss *assessor* – someone with expert knowledge of the insurance claims minefield to work on *your* behalf. Someone to fight your corner in an effort to maximise, rather than minimise, your claim. And because you may need them very quickly, it makes sense to find one now, rather than waiting until a loss adjuster makes an appearance.

Appropriate levels of insurance are undoubtedly important. But in order to gain the greatest advantage from our insurance, we need to know what we're covered for and what's likely to happen if we're unfortunate enough to need to claim.

Under cover?

'We're insured, so why do we need a business continuity plan?' is a more common question than you might think, particularly among smaller businesses (and some larger ones too, actually). And it's a reasonable question, if a tad naïve.

Granted, there are a number of insurance options that may help from a business continuity perspective, including business interruption, consequential loss and increased cost of working cover, among others. The question is, are they enough to save your business in the event of a major disruption? And the answer is usually a resounding 'no'.

Such policies may provide a safety net for your business if things go horribly wrong. But we should bear in mind that insurance only addresses (some of) the financial impacts of some of your risks – it merely provides a pre-defined sum of money in the event that a certain pre-defined risk occurs.

It almost certainly won't pay out immediately – in fact, experience has shown that insurance can take months, or even years, to pay out and that the claims process is often fraught with difficulties (strangely enough, paying out on claims isn't the favourite activity for most insurance companies!).

In the meantime, what it won't do is keep your business operating or protect your cash flow in the short term. It won't stop your customers going elsewhere or protect your market share. It won't protect your reputation or replace the goodwill you've painstakingly built up, possibly over a period of many years. And it's a sobering thought that the sums paid out are often less than anticipated, and often don't actually cover the full value of the losses incurred.

So it's vital that you clearly understand what your various insurance policies cover and, as importantly, what they don't, so that you can supplement your risk management strategy with other appropriate mitigation measures, such as a decent business continuity plan.

The appropriate use of insurance is an important weapon in your business continuity and risk management armoury, but it's a big mistake to view it as the only (or even the main) weapon. It should really be seen as the last line of defence, rather than the first.

Follow-up actions

This page is for you to note any tips from this chapter that struck a chord, along with the follow-up actions you intend to take to benefit your business continuity management programme in your organisation.

TIP/PAGE...	TO MAKE THIS TIP WORK FOR ME I WILL...

Chapter 4
Incident Management and Business Continuity Plans

Those who plan do better than those who do not plan, even though they rarely stick to their plan.

– attributed to WINSTON CHURCHILL

What's the use?

It may come as a shock to some – particularly those who championed or funded the development of their organisation's business continuity plan – but, despite the time and effort spent on them, most plans won't work!

Because most business continuity plans aren't designed to actually be used. They're designed to pass an audit. So they're crammed full of all the peripheral stuff that an auditor, quite reasonably, wants to see to prove that you've done things 'properly'. Which means there are often several dozen pages of scope, objectives, policy, assumptions, version control, maintenance, testing, business impact analysis, risk assessment and goodness knows what else before you get anywhere near the bit that actually helps you to deal with the crisis/incident/disaster/emergency (delete as applicable) that you're faced with. Does this sound familiar?

But we have to include all of that stuff in order to pass the audit, don't we? Well, to an extent, that's true – it probably has to be documented somewhere. The question is, where?

One option is to write two plans – one for the auditor and one for the people who might actually have to use it in anger. But that would almost certainly result in some duplication of effort, not to mention some awkward questions from said auditor if he rumbled you.

POWER TIP

A better option is to simply remove all of the peripheral information and put it into a separate document, which forms part of your overall business continuity management system. That way those called upon to put the plan into operation might actually be able to find the stuff they need, when they need it, rather than ploughing through pages and pages of 'stuff' first. Or, worse still, ignoring the plan completely, at precisely the time that it should be of most use.

Make yourself a tome

There can be a temptation to cram a business continuity plan with anything that might be vaguely useful in the event of its activation. After all, we don't know precisely what's going to hit us so we need to make sure the plan has everything in there that we might possibly need, don't we?

The trouble is that this tends to make the plan quite large. And one thing that's pretty much guaranteed to ensure your business continuity plan never gets read, lovingly crafted though it may have been, is to make it large and verbose.

There are several ways to keep the size of the plan down to sensible proportions. For instance:

➤ Using a style of writing that's concise and to the point. There's a time and place for flowery prose, but the business continuity plan really isn't it.

➤ Abbreviating where appropriate – beware of overdoing this, however, and do ensure that the people using the plan actually understand what the abbreviations and acronyms mean.

➤ Using checklists and action-oriented language, rather than huge tracts of text – 'Prepare for return to BAU' uses a lot less space (and ink) than 'As progress continues during the recovery operation, the team should be prepared to move back to the affected facility and resume normal business operations' (which, incidentally, came from a real plan!).

➤ Giving careful consideration to what should and shouldn't be documented in the plan. One old chestnut, for instance, is the fire evacuation procedure, which absolutely should not be in there (if people have to look in the business continuity plan when the alarm goes off to find out how to evacuate then someone's completely missed the point!). Likewise, standard operating procedures and the contents of the Yellow Pages may be better left out.

- Avoiding specific scenario-based plans, unless absolutely necessary – except maybe some very high-level ones, such as unavailability of premises, facilities, technology or people.
- Avoiding repetition – one copy of a map or contact list or whatever in the appendices, rather than multiple copies of the same thing in several sections.

Not only are weighty, wordy plans unlikely to be read before the event but, worse still, they're unlikely to be used at the time.

Bear in mind that the purpose of the plan is to aid the response, management and recovery teams in the event of an unexpected, difficult and potentially very stressful situation. What people really need at that point is something concise, action oriented and easy to use, not a huge, weighty tome that buries the pertinent bits in a mountain of unnecessary detail.

A numbers game

Most crisis or incident management plans contain lists of contact details (in fact some plans contain little else, but that's another story). Generally speaking this is a very good idea, as communication is, almost without fail, the biggest issue that a crisis or incident management team has to deal with. So anything that supports and eases that process is probably a good thing.

But there are a couple of issues to consider here...

Firstly, lists of phone numbers in our crisis management plans are only useful if a) they're correct and up to date and b) they relate to the key contacts that we need to communicate with during a crisis, particularly in the early stages. This might sound obvious, but some planners make the mistake of including the contact details of everyone they can think of, from key customers to toilet roll suppliers, and everyone in between. Much of this is unnecessary padding and only serves to make it more difficult to find the details that the team really needs.

Secondly, and more importantly, a list of contact numbers is not a crisis communication plan. A crisis communication plan includes, among other things, the identification of key stakeholders, an understanding of their needs during a crisis and a bit of thought about the messages that need to be communicated and the methods of doing so. That might mean the inclusion of some checklists of key actions or some pro forma statements that can be customised to meet the prevailing situation. Or not, depending on the preferences and the abilities of the team members. But it almost certainly means some education and awareness and exercising and testing if it's to be a proper, effective plan.

There's a balance to be struck between ensuring the plan contains sufficient information and reducing its effectiveness by including too much superfluous stuff. The bottom line, though, is that a list of phone numbers isn't really much of a plan.

A bag of spanners?

A question that comes up from time to time is what form the incident management and business recovery plans should take – should they be scenario based or generic? Some organisations favour the former and some the latter but, before you make the decision, there are some important considerations.

One method used by advocates of the scenario-based approach is to brainstorm every conceivable scenario and write a plan for each. Fires, floods, explosions, power failures, hurricanes, pandemics, plagues of locusts, you name it. And, in fairness, there may be some merit in that approach for *some* organisations. But all too often the end result is an awful lot of effort and a plan that runs to hundreds of pages that no one ever reads.

More importantly, the scenario that subsequently befalls the organisation in question often isn't one that they thought of at the brainstorming stage, so they don't actually have a plan for it. A few real examples of this include:

- ➤ a hydroelectric power company that had to shut down its plant because a whale had swum into its sluice
- ➤ a company that fell victim to an industrial-sized version of a well-known scam, ending up with a huge bill for a lousy resurfacing job on their car park and suffering threats of blockades and violence against their staff when they refused to pay
- ➤ an airport whose terminal building disappeared into a hole in the ground while they were all looking up watching for planes falling out of the sky.

The point is that there are disasters and disruptions waiting to bite us that we couldn't possibly second-guess before the event. And, therefore, the likelihood is that, if we go down the scenario planning route, we won't have a plan that fits the situation we find ourselves in. So we end up either trying to cobble together some sort of hybrid of the plans we did write, or we throw the whole lot away and wing it on the day, neither of which is particularly desirable.

POWER TIP

It may be (nay, almost certainly is) far better to have a more generic plan – with checklists that assist with specific issues (e.g. staff welfare, emergency services liaison, internal/external communication, relocation, supply chain management, salvage, etc., etc.) as opposed to specific scenarios – along with a well-briefed, well-trained, well-exercised incident management team that's capable of responding to and dealing with whatever scenario presents itself.

In other words, a plan that provides a toolkit to select from to fit the specifics of the situation you find yourself in. After all, if what you really need is a screwdriver, a bag of spanners – no matter how large or how many spanners it contains – isn't really much use.

A reasonable assumption?

There's no getting away from it, we have to make some assumptions when we're putting our business continuity strategies and plans together. And that's a perfectly reasonable thing to do.

But it's a good idea – in fact, if we want our plans to be robust and stand a chance of actually working, it's essential – to challenge and validate those assumptions from time to time to ensure they're reasonable.

Typical examples of assumptions that might need a bit of a reality check include:

➤ The people that we rely on to make our plans work will all be available and contactable when we need them. But most people do have lives outside of work. They go on holiday. They go out. They turn off their mobile phones. They have the occasional tipple. They change their phone numbers without telling anyone. They might even be personally affected by the incident that causes us to invoke our plans.

➤ People will be willing to travel long distances and work at a location miles away from their nearest and dearest for as long as we want them to. The reality is that some people can't or just plain won't. And for those who can and will, experience shows that the Dunkirk spirit typically only lasts about a week or so.

➤ Everyone can work quite happily from home for as long as we want them to. While many can, some people can't, for a multitude of reasons. They may not have sufficient or appropriate working space or facilities. They may have personal circumstances that make home working difficult or impossible. Their role may not lend itself to working in isolation, even with the availability of online collaboration tools. Their internet and/or mobile phone signal may be poor. They may just be the sort of person who needs personal contact. Whatever the reasons, home working, particularly if it goes on for any length of time, doesn't work for everyone.

➤ Our IT or business recovery plans will work, even though we've never tested them. It's well known (ask anyone who's done it) that many recoveries don't actually work very well on the first test as there are wrinkles (sometimes great gaping chasms!) that need to be ironed out.

➤ Our customers will cut us some slack because we have such a good relationship with them. The harsh reality is that, like the Dunkirk spirit, the sympathy vote can be short lived.

➤ People will do what it says in the plan. The reality is that the only thing we can expect is that people will do unexpected things!

Assumption is the mother of all foul-ups, particularly where assumptions haven't been validated. By all means make assumptions when you have to, but do revisit them from time to time to ensure that an invalid assumption doesn't invalidate your plans.

Keep it simple

Albert Einstein is often quoted, possibly spuriously, as having said 'Everything should be made as simple as possible, but not simpler'.*

Whether or not the quotation is 100% accurate, its sentiment is entirely applicable to the development of our business continuity plans.

Because many plans are overly complicated, confusing, verbose, difficult to navigate or full of superfluous information. Some plans are all of these things. At the other end of the scale, some plans are simplistic in the extreme, containing little or nothing, other than a few contact details, that's likely to be of any use in an incident management or business recovery situation.

There is, however, undoubtedly a middle ground that we should strive for. One that results in a business continuity plan that's concise, easy to follow, action oriented and which contains the key information – or clear pointers to it – that we're likely to need in the heat of a major incident, without any unnecessary padding.

Why not take an objective look at your existing plans and see where they fall on the simplicity spectrum? And if they're anywhere near either extreme, take a leaf out of Mr Einstein's book and see what you can do to make them as simple as possible – but not simpler.

---

* It seems that what Albert actually said (in a 1933 lecture, 'On the Method of Theoretical Physics') was 'It can scarcely be denied that the supreme goal of all theory is to make the irreducible basic elements as simple and as few as possible without having to surrender the adequate representation of a single datum of experience', which someone else paraphrased on the grounds that the original needed to be simplified!

A plan on a page

Ronald Reagan was allegedly famous for demanding that any document requiring his attention should be no longer than a single sheet of paper, and for refusing to read anything which didn't comply with this edict. Now, whatever you thought of old Ronnie, he did have a point.

Experience tells us that if a business continuity plan is too large, too complex or too difficult to find the bits we actually need, then quite simply it won't be used. And what's the point of spending time and effort writing a plan that isn't going to be used when it's needed?

A good business continuity plan isn't measured by weight or thickness. A good business continuity plan is measured by its usefulness and usability.

So keep it simple. Keep it short and to the point. Cut out the superfluous stuff and focus on what's really important.

And actually, you can get a fair amount of information on a single sheet of paper – particularly if you cheat a bit and use both sides!

Idiot proof

It's said that Napoleon used to have on his staff an 'idiot' – a low-ranking soldier of even lower intellect!

When putting together his battle plans, before presenting them to his generals Napoleon would present them to his idiot and ask him to explain what they meant. If the idiot couldn't understand them, Napoleon would revise and simplify the plans before presenting them to the intended audience. The theory was that if the idiot could understand the plans then his generals ought to be able to.

While in these politically correct times it's probably not wise to use the term 'idiot', why not take a leaf out of Napoleon's book and get someone less experienced, less technical or more junior to review your various business continuity plans and give you some feedback prior to issuing the final versions. This will almost certainly result in improvements to the plans in terms of clarity, simplicity and usability. In other words, it'll help you, just as it helped Napoleon, to make them 'idiot proof'.

The wheat from the chaff

Information is a key ingredient for effective crisis or incident management. Without it, decision-making is likely to be, at the very least, difficult and risk or error prone.

At times the crisis management team may find itself working with insufficient or incomplete information at its disposal. At other times, there may be a glut of information available, from a number of sources, including employees or other business contacts, eyewitnesses, the news media or social media channels, to name a few. Some of it may be reliable but some may be inaccurate, uncorroborated or based on rumour, speculation or false assumptions rather than hard facts.

It's important that our crisis management planning considers how to address this crucial issue. One option is to nominate an information management team, to monitor the various information sources and to analyse, filter, assess and present the resulting *intelligence* – as distinct from unprocessed information or data – in a format that gives the decision-makers improved situational awareness and enables them to make more informed decisions.

Sorting the wheat from the chaff isn't easy and can take a fair amount of effort. But it's quicker and more efficient if the right machinery is put in place and operated by people who know how to use it effectively.

The soft option – part 1

There are a number of business continuity software tools on the market, some of which claim to simplify the planning process or even to do it all for you! And while there can be advantages in using such software (e.g. for a large organisation with numerous plans to maintain and dedicated business continuity staff to do it) for many businesses there are a number of distinct disadvantages. These include:

➤ Cost: some software is extremely expensive, often with an ongoing annual maintenance fee on top of the purchase price.

➤ Training: more often than not, users have to be trained before the software can be put to use. And, because the software is used infrequently, refresher courses are often required. The training overhead (and the associated cost) can be significant. Or worse still, the business continuity manager ends up maintaining everyone's plans for them – the exact opposite of what most business continuity managers want!

➤ Inflexibility: often the package and its associated methodology, rather than the user, dictates the format of the plans produced. The resulting plans are sometimes large, containing lots of repeated or superfluous data, or not particularly user friendly, resulting in them being difficult to use (or, worse still, ignored) when it really matters, i.e. when trying to use them for real.

It may be that you have a compelling reason for using software, and that the advantages outweigh the disadvantages. So by all means look into whether or not it's right for you. But don't make the mistake of thinking that software will do all the work for you – it won't. And don't be fooled into thinking that a software package is a substitute for knowledge or experience. Think about it – in the same way that buying a copy of Word won't make you into an instant novelist, buying a business continuity planning software package won't guarantee a business continuity plan that's any good.

The soft option – part 2

Having majored on the disadvantages of business continuity software tools in the previous tip, this one aims to redress the balance a little. Because one distinct advantage that some software tools have over the more 'traditional' word processor-based plan is that they provide mobile app capability, allowing the plans to be viewed and easily navigated on a mobile phone or tablet.

It's true that it's eminently possible to save a Word-based plan (other word processors are available!) as a PDF file that can be stored on or accessed via a mobile device. However, it can be difficult, if not nigh-on impossible, to read and navigate through what's typically a fairly lengthy and complex document if it hasn't been carefully formatted to be read on a screen not much larger than your hand. And if it has, it probably doesn't lend itself to being read on larger screens.

Mobile app-based plans are more likely to be structured so as to be easy to view and simple to navigate, via menus and links, rather than the endless scrolling that's more typical when trying to read a 'traditional' plan on a mobile phone.

The downside is that this comes at a cost. But as the saying goes 'you pays your money and you takes your choice'.

A premium quality business continuity plan?

A question that's sometimes asked of the business continuity manager is 'Will our business continuity plan get us a discount on our insurance premiums?'.

Sadly, the answer is almost always 'no'. It might help you get cover in the first place, as some insurers may refuse to provide certain types of insurance without evidence of a robust risk management and/or business continuity capability, but it's quite rare (though not completely unheard of) to get a significant discount just because you have a business continuity plan.

However, your business continuity plan or, more to the point, your business continuity *capability*, might work to your advantage in other ways. Because it should help you to understand what levels of cover you need, particularly on your business interruption insurance.

A robust business continuity capability could reduce your potential losses and enable you to get back to normal quicker, in which case you might save money by choosing a lower level of cover in the form of a shorter indemnity period and/or a reduced level of insured losses.

There's a big fat caveat, however, that you ignore at your peril. You need to have complete confidence in your business continuity capability, which, as we've discussed previously, isn't the same as merely having a business continuity plan.

But, of course, you do anyway – don't you?

Follow-up actions

This page is for you to note any tips from this chapter that struck a chord, along with the follow-up actions you intend to take to benefit your business continuity management programme in your organisation.

TIP/PAGE...	TO MAKE THIS TIP WORK FOR ME I WILL...

Chapter 5
Crisis/Incident Management

Don't panic.

> – Douglas Adams, *The Hitchhiker's Guide to the Galaxy* (1979)

Crisis, what crisis?

The importance of effective crisis management cannot be overstated. But if we're going to effectively manage a crisis, we really ought to know when we're having one!

The characteristics of a crisis include:

- an urgent need for decisions
- a lack of accurate information on which to base those decisions
- an acute shortage of time
- insufficient resources at our disposal
- uncertainty of the outcome.

You could argue that for some organisations this is business as usual! But we're not talking about day-to-day glitches or management headaches here. Crisis management is about dealing with extreme situations – stuff that's outside the scope of normal business problems; that potentially threatens life and limb or the future of the business; that's outside the scope of 'normal' management experience.

Managing a crisis is not the same as normal day-to-day business management. It needs specific skills and abilities. It needs sufficiently trained and experienced people. And it needs skills, training and rehearsal if it's to be effective.

So make sure your crisis management team members are sufficiently senior, up to the job and prepared for it should a real crisis ever strike.

Opportunity knocks

It's often said, albeit somewhat spuriously, that when written in Chinese the word 'crisis' is made up of two characters, one representing danger and the other representing opportunity. Whether that's strictly true or not, it raises an interesting question in relation to our crisis management planning. The question is, when faced with some kind of crisis, rather than just focusing on the negative aspects, should we also be looking for any positive opportunities that we might be able to take advantage of?

For instance, while the thought of talking to the media in a crisis may be seen by some as difficult and dangerous, there's potentially a huge opportunity to gain some positive PR (or, at the very least, to avoid some negative PR). Indeed, a number of organisations have done so to great effect when dealing with their own crises.

There may well be other opportunities too. Such as opportunities to restructure parts of the organisation, discontinue unprofitable elements of the business, move to new premises, implement improvements to the infrastructure, identify and reward talent and commitment, change our processes, demonstrate good leadership… or whatever.

The point is that, while there will undoubtedly be some difficult and possibly dangerous aspects to dealing with a crisis, there will often be some positive opportunities there too.

So, whether or not we believe the above interpretation of the Chinese characters for crisis, the least we should do is to look for the opportunities. Because if we don't look we're unlikely to find them, in which case we're even less likely to benefit from them.

An issue with authority

In line with accepted best practice, most organisations' business continuity arrangements will include some kind of crisis or incident management team, which is responsible for managing the response to and recovery from a major disruptive incident.

However, the seniority of the personnel making up this important team varies significantly from organisation to organisation. In some, the team comprises directors or senior executives; in others it's senior managers, such as departmental heads. Often, it's a combination. Sometimes, team membership is delegated further down the hierarchy.

Whatever the make-up of this key team, it can only operate effectively if it's able to actually make decisions, some of which may result in significant financial, operational, legal or other commitments. It therefore either needs to include people who are senior enough to make those types of decisions or be given the authority to do so in certain situations. In the latter case, this delegated authority really needs to be agreed in advance, rather than trying to sort it out after an incident has occurred.

In the heat of the response to a crisis or major incident, the people trying to manage it need to be able to get on with things. The last thing they need is delays caused by them having to refer every decision upwards.

A leading role

A crisis or incident management team needs a leader – that's pretty much a given. So the obvious thing to do is to give the role to the most senior person in the organisation. And, as often as not, that's exactly what happens – the CEO is nominated as the person to head up the incident management team. But is that the right decision?

The problem is that the CEO often has some quite important other stuff to do. Like talking to the media or other key stakeholders, for instance. Which, let's face it, is a big enough task in its own right, without adding to it the equally big task of managing the crisis or incident.

And anyway, what people want most from their leaders in a crisis is leadership. So we might be better off getting our glorious leader to act like one and, as importantly, to be seen to be doing so. By putting themselves about – talking to, encouraging and motivating employees, helping them to stay focused on what's really important. By demonstrating that they're taking a personal interest in, and responsibility for, the care of those affected and ensuring that their needs are met. By communicating with the various interested parties, such as employees, customers, neighbours, business partners, investors, shareholders, the media and other key stakeholders.

While the crisis or incident management team might appreciate a bit of leadership too, it's a teeny bit difficult to display that leadership to the rest of the organisation if the CEO is hidden away in the incident control centre. Much better then to give them a role that enables them to be visible and to do what, at least in theory, they're best at.

The magnificent seven

Theory has it that the ideal size for a team or a working group is seven people (see References). Above that, the group will tend to split into smaller groups – a phenomenon that can be readily observed wherever there's a gathering of more than seven friends, associates or team-mates, whether it's in a social or a work situation.

It's also been said that, in a meeting or work group, each additional member above seven reduces the likelihood of making good, quick, executable decisions by ten per cent. Once you hit 16 or 17 people, therefore, the team's potential for effective decision-making is close to zero.

It stands to reason then, that a crisis or incident management team with more than seven members is likely to be less effective, from a decision-making perspective, than one with seven members or fewer. So it would seem to make sense to limit the membership of such a team, or at least the core, decision-making element of it.

That doesn't, however, mean that other key people should be ignored. By all means include subject matter experts or other interested parties in meetings intended to disseminate information or engender discussion or feedback. When it comes to the knottier issue of decision-making, though – particularly in a crisis situation, where critical decisions may have to be made quickly – seven may well be the magic number.

Perhaps there's a reason why the Magnificent Seven got their name. The Average Eight or the Ineffective Eleven doesn't have quite the same ring to it!

Tempus fugit

There's a well-known saying that 'time flies when you're having fun'. But time also flies when you're up against it and an acute shortage of time is one of the characteristics of a crisis (see 'Crisis, what crisis?' on page 90).

Effective crisis or incident management is largely about getting on top of the situation as quickly as possible; making key decisions, particularly in the early stages, that really make a difference. Because, unsurprisingly, the quicker we start to get a grip on the situation and begin to exert some influence and control, the more likelihood there is of a successful resolution. And, guess what, the longer we take to get on top of things the more we find ourselves reacting to events rather than having any influence over them and the likelihood of any sort of success dwindles.

The early period of a crisis is sometimes referred to as 'the golden hour' – in reality it may be several hours or it may be just a few minutes, depending on the particular crisis – but it's the time when the key decisions that we make (or don't make) have a huge impact on the outcome.

Those involved in the crisis or incident management team need to be able to get stuck in quickly and make things happen. So they need to have the tools and the authority to make decisions and be able to do so quickly and effectively under pressure. They need to know what's expected of them and they need to be prepared. So they need to be adequately trained and they need to have rehearsed.

'Procrastination is the thief of time' is another well-known saying. But procrastination is also the enemy of effective crisis management and something the crisis or incident management team can't afford. So it's not good enough to merely have a plan. Those involved in crisis or incident management need to have the capability to go with it.

The deciding factor

While effective decision-making is often linked to the quality and accuracy of available information (see 'The wheat from the chaff' on page 83 and 'Questioning the answers' on page 101), another important, though often overlooked, consideration is 'decision fatigue'.

Decision fatigue refers to the fact that the more decisions we have to make, the worse the quality of those decisions tends to become. And the phenomenon is generally thought to be linked to the number, rather than the importance, of those decisions. Much like muscle fatigue, if the 'decision muscle' is exercised too frequently, it will tire and weaken and will eventually fail. Decision fatigue is exacerbated when the decision-maker is tired or when glucose levels are low.

By definition, our crisis or incident management teams contain decision-makers (if yours doesn't, you should seriously question whether the right people are in it!). So these people, who are often required to make numerous challenging, thought-provoking decisions in their business-as-usual roles, may be called upon to make critical decisions in a crisis context. And, depending when the crisis happens (towards the end of a busy day, for instance), they may have to do so when they've already used up their decision-making 'quota', in which case their ability to make quality decisions may be impaired. Worse still, 'decision inertia' can set in, whereby decisions are delayed or not made at all.

The best remedy for decision fatigue is the same as for any other type of fatigue – rest. The importance of alternatives or deputies to the primary crisis or incident management team members cannot, therefore, be overstated. Most of us have our own 'war stories' about how we worked 24, 36, 48 hours or more at a stretch – what we almost always neglect to mention is how effective our decision-making and our ability to think rationally was by the end!

Other tactics for combating decision fatigue include ensuring that we eat properly and stay hydrated, along with minimising the number of unimportant or trivial decisions we have to make, by delegating or allowing someone else to decide for us. Barack Obama is often quoted as saying 'I don't want to make decisions about what I'm eating or wearing, because I have too many other decisions to make'. Agreeing predetermined actions for certain triggers or using structured decision-making processes or tools can also help.

While we may like to think we're superhuman, actually most of us aren't and decision fatigue is something that we all suffer from from time to time. So it's important to recognise it as a potentially limiting factor in crisis management and consider ways to avoid it or minimise it. The best time to make those decisions, however, is probably not when we're in crisis decision-making mode!

Log it or lose it

Most people with a role in an incident management or business recovery team accept that, if they have to invoke their plans, it's a good idea to keep an event log. Indeed, many plans contain a pre-prepared event logging form for just such a purpose, with headings such as date, time, event, response and so forth. Which is a good start.

The problem is that most of us just don't record enough information. We might feel we've captured enough for our own internal post-incident review, but we seldom consider the other possibilities. Like having to justify our actions in support of an insurance claim, or defend our actions or decisions in the event of legal action, or an inquest or public inquiry. To put it another way, we don't record enough information to cover our backside!

When you consider that most court cases, inquiries and inquests take place a long time – sometimes several years – after the event, you can see why relying on our memories isn't really good enough. Some of us can't remember what we did last week, let alone recall in detail what we did and why we did it on a given day several years ago.

POWER TIP

So what is enough information? As well as recording events and actions it's important to record decisions, the reasons for and the reasoning behind those decisions, the context in which they were made (such as time or other pressures), the options considered, the information or advice available at the time, who was involved, whether and when the actions were carried out, the timescales involved (how long it took, not just the time it was completed), and any review or revision that was subsequently undertaken.

This may seem like overkill now, but don't underestimate its importance. And if you ever find yourself in the unfortunate position of having to defend your actions in court, you'll be glad you took note – and took adequate notes, in the form of a detailed event and decision log.

What's the story?

'Log it or lose it' on the previous page highlighted the importance of event and decision logging, largely from the standpoint of being able to justify, or defend, our actions at a later date.

But this isn't the only reason for event logging. And the detailed event/decision log, containing all the things suggested in that previous tip (such as reasoning, context, options considered, information/advice available, etc.) isn't the only kind of log that has value.

Yes, it's important to have all of that detail available to refer back to at a later date. But a concise, high-level log of the main issues, decisions made and actions planned, writ large on flipcharts or whiteboards, or, for the more technically minded, displayed on a computer screen*, can help the crisis or incident management team immensely during the heat of battle.

This type of high-level event log provides a 'storyboard' to keep all team members up to speed with what's happened so far and what needs to be done. It helps the team to remain focused on the important stuff. And it's particularly useful at handover times or when there's a need to brief someone who hasn't been all that involved so far – for instance when those pesky executives come asking questions.

In the context of crisis or incident management, a short story can have as much impact as the event logging equivalent of *War and Peace*.

---

* Whichever medium you choose, do make sure you have a backup copy. In the case of flipcharts or whiteboards, a quick photograph before removal can help ensure you don't lose valuable information that might be needed in the days/weeks/months/years to come.

Feel the rhythm

Every business has a rhythm. The daily production meeting, the weekly sales meeting, the CEO's fortnightly morale-boosting email, the monthly team briefing, and so forth, all contribute to this business rhythm.

The military, particularly in wartime, has a thing called the 'battle rhythm', which, depending on your choice of dictionary (here, taken from Wiktionary), may be defined as 'A daily routine or order of business, especially as assumed by a military organisation or during crisis'.

While most businesses aren't structured or run in the same way as the armed forces, the concept of battle rhythm can certainly be applied to crisis or incident management. Because it's largely about information management and communication. It's about implementing effective processes for gathering, assimilating and communicating information, providing situational awareness to the decision-makers to help them make informed decisions, and ensuring the right information is communicated to the relevant stakeholders at the appropriate times.

The crisis management battle rhythm includes the frequency of briefing meetings, situation reports, updates, stakeholder communications, and so on. That frequency may well vary as events unfold, as circumstances change and as our responses enable us to get on top of the situation. It's likely that the tempo will be quite high in the early stages but will usually reduce as time goes by and things become calmer – a bit like starting with a quickstep and finishing with a waltz!

But our crisis management battle rhythm shouldn't be left to chance, or be driven entirely by external factors. By considering in 'peacetime', through planning and exercising, the tempos we'd want to adopt in 'wartime', at what stages, and how we might go about setting them, we're much more likely to have control over the rhythm, rather than dancing to someone else's tune!

Questioning the answers

'The wheat from the chaff' on page 83 suggests setting up an information management team to aid the crisis management team's situational awareness, thus helping them to make more informed decisions.

In order to do so effectively, there are five simple questions that such a team should be constantly asking:
POWER TIP

1. **What do we know?** It's important to distinguish between confirmed facts and rumour, speculation or assumption.

2. **How do we know?** Did we hear first hand from a reliable source? Has the information been corroborated? How confident are we that it's true and accurate?

3. **What don't we know?** We sometimes have to admit that there are things that we just don't know, rather than trying to fill the gaps with guesswork.

4. **What would we like to know?** What crucial pieces of information are we missing and what is the impact of not knowing?

5. **How can we find out?** What information sources can we tap into? What are the primary sources and what other sources can we use to confirm the information is correct?

The answers to these questions will help ensure that information passed to the decision-makers is accurate, validated and fit for purpose.

In order to make absolutely sure, however, it's as important to question the answers as it is to answer the questions.

Fight, flight or film

The 'fight or flight' reflex (sometimes expanded to 'fight, flight or freeze') is a well-known expression describing the instinctive physiological response to a threatening situation. It's been an important part of the human make-up since our distant ancestors had to deal with the occasional unscheduled meeting with a sabre-toothed tiger or other predator.

Recently, though, and perhaps somewhat worryingly, another 'f' seems to have been added, the 'f' in question standing for 'film'. Rather than preparing to fight or running away from danger, some people nowadays choose to stay and record events on their smartphones. And the phenomenon seems to be on the increase.

From a crisis or incident management point of view, this raises a couple of serious implications that merit some consideration.

First, following some kind of major incident some of the people we're responsible for may be unwittingly putting themselves in danger, potentially adding to the people issues that we have to deal with.

Second, many of the resulting recordings are posted on various social media platforms and/or shared with the news media, in some cases within minutes of the event happening or even live streamed. Which means that all kinds of people will get to see them, including, potentially, our employees, customers and other stakeholders.

Whatever your personal opinion of the merits of this behaviour, it happens. So it's something that your crisis or incident management team should, at the very least, be aware of and perhaps your HR people should counsel employees against.

A question of focus

'Questioning the answers' on page 101 suggests a few key questions for an information management team, supporting the crisis or incident management team, to ask.

This tip suggests some questions for the crisis/incident management team itself to ask at its regular review sessions, to ensure it keeps its collective eye on the ball, broken down into four important categories:

- Current situation: what are the main issues now? What's changed?
- Strategic intent: what's the most important strategic objective that we need to focus on achieving?
- Actions: what specific actions are we going to take in order to achieve our strategic intent?
- Responsibilities: who's going to carry out which activities?

And don't forget those two small but important questions 'What if?' and 'So what?'[4], which can be so helpful in identifying the potential consequences of a decision or event that hasn't yet happened.

Follow-up actions

This page is for you to note any tips from this chapter that struck a chord, along with the follow-up actions you intend to take to benefit your business continuity management programme in your organisation.

TIP/PAGE...	TO MAKE THIS TIP WORK FOR ME I WILL...

Chapter 6
Crisis Communications

The key to an effective response to a major or catastrophic incident is communication.

> – **London Assembly Report of the 7 July Review Committee** (2006)

A matter of perception

As suggested in 'Crisis, what crisis?' on page 90, effective crisis management needs a mechanism for spotting that you're having one in the first place and a capable team of people who are able to make decisions and take appropriate actions to deal with the situation. And this is the focus of attention for many crisis management plans.

But the importance of being *seen* to be taking the right actions and being *heard* to say the right things is sometimes overlooked, or not given the focus that it warrants.

The 'audience' (including your various stakeholders) observing the crisis from the outside will make their decisions on how well (or otherwise) a crisis is handled based on their perception, which may or may not reflect reality. But their perception *is* their reality, and it's created by what they see and what they hear.

In addition to the mechanics of how a crisis will be managed and by whom, effective crisis management needs to give due consideration to reputation management. And reputation management needs effective perception management. Which means a properly thought out communications strategy, along with tools to deliver it effectively.

In fact, perception management is arguably *the* most important element of your crisis management planning.

The big issue

When dealing with any kind of crisis or major incident, one of the biggest issues you're likely to face is communication – whether that's internal communication with your own people or external communication with your customers, suppliers, shareholders, neighbours, the media or whoever.

Get this aspect of your crisis management right and you'll make life easier (or, at least, less difficult) for yourself. Get it wrong and you'll almost certainly multiply your problems several-fold. Get it right and you stand a fighting chance of coming through with your reputation intact – perhaps even enhanced. Get it wrong and your reputation can be shredded in a moment – or a soundbite.

All of which suggests that you should give some thought in advance to your crisis communication strategy and plans rather than trying to wing it on the day. This includes an understanding of your various stakeholders and their concerns, so you can decide how and what to communicate, and to whom.

So why not take some time out to identify your key audiences and the types of messages that you might want to get across to each; and have a think about the appropriate mechanisms for doing so and how and when you might deploy them?

POWER TIP

Far better to do that groundwork now than trying to work it out when your back's against the wall.

A hotline to your staff

It's probably an understatement to say that in the wake of a major incident, the crisis or incident management team tends to have plenty to think about and do. And their thought processes aren't necessarily helped very much by everyone in the organisation, however concerned or well meaning they might be, trying to contact them to find out what's happened, what's going on now, whether they can help, what they should do, and so on.

One tried and tested and extremely effective way of helping to reduce the volume of incoming calls is to implement an incident hotline. Typically, this consists of a voicemail-based service, whereby the incident management team has one number that they call to leave messages periodically, and staff at large have a second number that they call to listen to those messages.

There are other bells and whistles that can be bolted on, such as the ability for staff members to leave their own message in reply, but the hotline doesn't need to be particularly sophisticated for it to be a really useful tool – for disseminating small amounts of relatively basic information to a large number of people, with a small amount of effort.

Of course, there are one or two important considerations – like ensuring that the hotline can handle an adequate number of concurrent calls and isn't affected by the incident (hence many organisations use an external service rather than doing it themselves); or making sure that all staff (including the incident management team) know the hotline number and how and when to use it; and testing it periodically to make sure it actually works – but these pale into insignificance compared with the potential reduction in grief that a hotline can bring.

So if you don't already have one, why not consider implementing an incident hotline as part of your crisis communications strategy?

The social club

The world is changing. More specifically, as regards this tip, the way that people communicate is changing.

For instance, the comparatively recent phenomenon of social media has become part of many people's normal mix of communication methods. For the social media generation, even email is becoming old hat and these days they're just as likely to communicate via Facebook, Snapchat, Instagram, Twitter, WhatsApp or whatever the latest trend is.

So if the way we communicate is changing, are our crisis communications strategies and plans also changing to take account of this new world? Have we considered, for example, the potential for using social media in a business continuity or crisis management context? And if so, how?

The jury's still out on how useful or effective social networking sites, blogs, tweets, instant messaging, etc. might be for things like awareness-raising or education, or progress reporting/monitoring as part of the business continuity management programme, but a number of organisations are now using them for crisis communications.

While social media might not be everyone's cup of tea (or perhaps you're more inclined towards a skinny latte nowadays), you might consider the following:

➤ setting up a closed user group on WhatsApp, LinkedIn, or other appropriate platform(s), for communicating with colleagues, customers, suppliers or other stakeholders

➤ using Facebook, Twitter, blogs, etc. to communicate with your stakeholders, for instance by circulating articles, strategies, thoughts or questions

➤ monitoring relevant social media platforms for negative PR posted by those with an axe to grind and using them to put your side of the story across.

Clearly there are a number of considerations to get our heads around, not least of which are the security aspects of utilising what are, by definition, mostly public forums. Even with secure 'closed' groups there is a risk of what is said going outside the group (via screenshots, for instance), so you should make sure anything you say in a closed group cannot be held against you if it gets out.

As with any other communications media, we need to identify our key audiences and the messages that we want to get across, then select the appropriate vehicles for doing so and think carefully about how we deploy them. This is likely to comprise a wide variety of media, from phones to Facebook, email to adverts, text messages to tweets – and whatever else works for you.

Like it or not, social media in one form or another is well and truly with us and is probably here to stay (at least until the next new thing comes along). If we write it off because we personally don't use it, or if we simply choose to ignore it, we do so at our peril.

Deal or no deal

Dealing with the media is an issue that often crops up in the context of crisis or incident management. To many, this translates as dealing with (or trying to avoid!) the journalists who are looking for interviews or comments and the pressure that we often feel when doing so.

But this is largely missing the point. Because 'dealing with the media' isn't actually about dealing with the media per se – it's about communicating with our stakeholders. And if we get past our fear or paranoia, the media, in their various forms, can provide a powerful conduit for doing this.

POWER TIP

So rather than thinking about how to 'deal with' the media, we should change the focus to one of using the media to help communicate our messages to our various audiences.

Clearly our spokespeople need to be adequately trained and prepared in media communication techniques. But to use the media effectively, we need to give at least as much consideration to identifying who our stakeholders are, what their concerns might be and which media might influence their thinking, so that we can craft our messages accordingly (using the tried and tested 'CARE' technique*, of course).

The media are not the audience. But they can be hugely influential and are, therefore, a potentially important route to the people who really matter. So if we worry a bit less about how we're going to 'deal with' the media and a bit more about how best to *engage* with them to get our messages across, we can actually use them to our advantage.

---

* CARE stands for **C**oncern, **A**ction and **Re**assurance. Remembering it can help spokespeople to show concern, demonstrate that their organisation is on top of the situation and put their audience's minds at rest without getting into detail about the prevailing situation.[5]

No news is bad news

There are two common misconceptions about the media that are all too commonly offered by incident management teams as a reason for not talking to them.

The first is that the media won't be interested in their organisation, either because it's not a household name or because they think that their problems wouldn't be particularly newsworthy.

The second is that if they avoid the media they'll go away and leave them alone.

Unfortunately, they're likely to be spectacularly wrong on both counts.

As regards the first point, the reality is that it's the media, not the crisis-struck organisation, that gets to decide whether a story is newsworthy or not (see 'In search of the TRUTH' on the next page).

On the second point, that might actually be partly right – at least for a while. The trouble is that while they're 'away' the media are unlikely to be leaving you alone. They're more likely to be talking to someone else – quite probably someone with a different agenda to yours, who's more than happy to share their thoughts with a media hungry for an interesting soundbite or two.

The point here is that if the media take an interest in you, a strategy of ignoring them probably isn't a particularly sensible one.

And in any case, why wouldn't you take the opportunity to put your side of the story across, to communicate with your key audiences, to show concern and show that you're in control?

To quote C. Northcote Parkinson,[6] 'The vacuum caused by a failure to communicate is soon filled with rumour, misrepresentation, drivel and poison.'

In other words, trying to avoid the media when they're looking for a story is unlikely to be one of your better decisions.

In search of the TRUTH

'No news is bad news' on the previous page suggested that it's the media, not the crisis-struck organisation, that gets to decide whether a story is newsworthy or not. But how exactly do they decide?

Well, it's quite simple really: journalists are looking for the 'TRUTH'.

Before you fall off your chair or start to rant and rave in disagreement, there's something important about the TRUTH in this context that you need to know. And that's the fact that the word TRUTH is an acronym that provides a guide to what a journalist sees as news.

T stands for **Topical**. A story is topical if it's 'of the moment'. So your story might be more newsworthy because it fits with a prevailing theme or if a link can be made with something else that's currently in the news.

R is for **Relevant**. Relevant to the journalist's audience, that is. This may be a particular age group, gender, interest, lifestyle, demographic or geographical area, among other things.

U stands for **Unusual**. If it's out of the ordinary (and most crises are, by definition), a journalist is likely to be interested.

T is for **Trouble**. Yes it's true, journalists do like conflict. Because, quite often, their readers, viewers or listeners find a bit of conflict interesting too.

H stands for **Human**. Journalists like stories about people. So if people are affected in some way, there's probably a story in it.

For a journalist, the ideal story will contain all of the above elements. But they may be happy with three or four of them, particularly if it's a proverbial 'slow news day'.

So, while you might think your crisis isn't particularly newsworthy, running it through the 'TRUTH' test might give you a different perspective and, importantly, allow you to plan your response accordingly.

Making a statement?

Many organisations shy away from speaking to the media at times of crisis (see 'The fear factor' on page 115), thinking that a written statement will do the job just as well. But issuing a written statement rather than putting forward a spokesperson is a risky strategy.

Written statements have a limited effect. While they're fine on social media in the first hour or so, relying on a written statement as your only form of communication means you lose much of your control over the message. Because a reporter will edit your statement, usually down to a single paragraph, and will read it out on air in their tone of voice rather than yours, which is unlikely to sound sympathetic to your cause.

Organisations need to be seen to engage with their key audiences in a crisis. While written statements are better than nothing, at best they only provide an 'arm's-length' message, which doesn't do anything to enable that vital engagement.

The fear factor

One of the most stress-inducing aspects of crisis or incident management is the dreaded media interview. Normally unflappable executives and seasoned presenters have been known to break into a cold sweat, or even to beat a hasty retreat at the prospect.

It's only natural to be nervous in such a situation. Strangely enough, there's a good chance that the journalist will be nervous too, which is quite a sobering thought. And nerves aren't necessarily a bad thing, as any half-decent presenter or performer will tell you. Nerves can keep you focused, keep you on your toes and give you an edge.

Fear, however, isn't good. Fear can turn the most polished of performers into a blubbering or blabbering wreck. Or cause them to run away. While there can, in some circumstances, be valid reasons for refusing to engage with the media, fear is the most common one, although few will actually admit it.

But fear is usually the result of being outside your comfort zone, often because of a lack of knowledge or experience. So preparation is the key. It's amazing how many nominated crisis media spokespeople have never had any proper crisis media training, or who went on a course many years ago but have subsequently never had a refresher or practised what they learned. It's hardly surprising, therefore, that the thought of facing a potentially hostile journalist 'in anger' fills them with dread.

While it's unlikely, and probably undesirable, that the butterflies will ever completely disappear, it is eminently possible to get rid of the fear – through training and regular practice, whether that's through rehearsal or doing it for real. Experience builds confidence and confidence kills fear.

So what do you reckon your media spokepeople would rather be – scared or prepared?

Three-point turn

When an organisation finds itself in the media spotlight, it's not unusual for the person put forward as spokesperson, however senior they are, to be nervous about being drawn into answering questions that they'd rather not answer.

Clearly this person really ought to have had some crisis media training *before* the event but, unfortunately, this isn't always the case.

A technique that can help enormously in the cut and thrust of a hostile media interview is to think, before entering the fray, of three (and only three) points that you want to get across, to rehearse them and to stick to them during the interview. You'll need to give careful consideration to your three points, but they should probably focus on:

1. **Concern** for the people involved

2. The fact that you've **activated** your pre-prepared plan

3. **Reassurance** that everything's under control.

...in other words, the 'CARE' message alluded to in 'Deal or no deal' on page 111.

This can help enormously in focusing the spokesperson's mind and in wrestling control back from an aggressive interviewer. Whenever an awkward question is asked, rather than getting flustered or drawn into answering it, they can simply fall back on their three points, perhaps saying something like 'That's not the important thing here – what is important is…' and repeating one (or more) of them.

And if you want proof, next time you see a politician or other media savvy person being grilled, just take a look at how well they execute their three-point turn.

As easy as ABC

If you've given some thought to your crisis communications plan, you've no doubt nominated some media spokespeople – you may even be one. So one day you might find yourself on the receiving end of a journalist's questions. And if you're not overly experienced in this situation, the temptation might be to just answer them.

But dealing effectively with the media isn't actually about answering their questions – it's about saying what *you* want to say. And the two things are often very different, as the journalist and you are likely to have very different agendas.

So how exactly do you go about not answering a journalist's questions?

First, and this may sound obvious, you need to know what you do want to say. So you need to prepare. You probably won't get much thinking time during the interview, so you need to have done your thinking beforehand (see 'Three-point turn' on page 116).

Secondly, when faced with a journalist's questions, you can use the 'ABC rule'.

A is for **Acknowledge**: This is your initial response to the question that's been asked. Rather than just blatantly ignoring it, you might say something like 'That's a very interesting question...'

B is for **Bridge**: This is where you build a link to what you want to say, rather than just answering the question. You might say something like 'Before I answer that I'd just like to say...' or 'The most important thing is...'

C is for **Content**: Now that you've built the bridge to what you want to say, here's where you get to communicate the content of *your* message.

It sounds easy, and with a bit of practice it can be. We've all seen people who are really good at this (although we hate them for it!) and who do it all the time. Yes, that's right: politicians. Think about it – when did you last hear a politician actually answer a question?

Politicians aside, following the ABC rule will help to put you, rather than the interviewer, in control and enable you to get *your* message across, no matter what questions they ask you.

Who cares?

'No news is bad news' (page 112) and 'The fear factor' (page 115) explore the wisdom of trying to avoid the media in a crisis and the (often spurious or misguided) reasons cited for doing so.

One common, if uninformed, reason given for not speaking to the media is the belief that the media are malicious and have it in for us; they're out to get us; they're actively looking to catch us out.

But this isn't actually true. The truth is, in fact, far more dangerous! The truth is that they don't care about you.

All the media really care about is having something interesting to report to their viewers, listeners or readers. And they really couldn't care less whether it paints you in a good light or a bad one, just as long as it's interesting.

The thing is, knowing this gives you a huge advantage. Because if you can give the media something positive, that paints you or your organisation in a good light as well as being interesting, then everyone's a winner.

Give them what they want and they'll be happy. Avoid them and they'll just go somewhere else for their input, in which case they're as likely to write a negative story as a positive one. In which case, they'll still be happy. The chances are, though, that you won't.

The media don't care. The question is, do you?

Breaking with tradition

Those of more mature years grew up with the 'traditional' news media – radio, TV and newspapers. We knew who the main players were and, while we might not have liked some of the reporting, the media's behaviour was, by and large, relatively predictable and followed, to a greater or lesser degree, a code of conduct.

But times have changed and the previously accepted norms no longer apply. One of the most fundamental changes is that the media landscape is no longer owned by the aforementioned traditional, once mainstream, media; it's now owned by the public. The prevalence of social media, coupled with smart devices that can record events and instantly upload or livestream them, means we can now all be 'citizen journalists' and anyone with an opinion or an axe to grind can be heard, pretty much immediately and say pretty much anything they want, often without corroboration. And the resulting 'news reports' can spread at an alarming rate, often before the traditional media have even begun reporting. Indeed, the traditional media now often get much of their information on an unfolding event via social media.

Unfortunately, many crisis communications plans haven't kept pace with these changes, still focusing mainly on the traditional media channels and the traditional methods of dealing with them, which severely hampers their ability to respond quickly enough in today's world. The excuse usually given is that they 'don't really do social media', which may be OK from a day-to-day business point of view, but it doesn't stop those who do use it to report on, highlight or add fuel to a crisis.

It's been suggested that it takes organisations an average of 21 hours to make any meaningful external communications after a crisis, whereas a social media storm can occur within minutes. The potential implications of this should be obvious – if they're not, some up-to-date media training should be seriously considered.

Whether we like it or not, and whether or not we use it in a day-to-day business context, social media in its various forms is now the mainstream for news reporting and consumption, so from a crisis management point of view, we absolutely need to acknowledge and learn about it and develop strategies and plans for dealing with the issues it can bring.

POWER TIP

'I MEAN' to say

When faced with the dreaded media interview (see 'The fear factor' on page 115), it should go without saying that preparation is key to success. But where to start? An effective method is the 'I MEAN' approach, where:

I = Idea. Ensure you have an agenda, so you don't end up following the interviewer's. A clear idea of what your business objective is when you give the interview is essential. It's also a good idea to consider who is the best spokesperson for this particular interview.

M = Message. It may sound obvious, but you need to have something to say. Decide on the key points that you want to get across to this particular audience, so you don't end up just answering the interviewer's questions (see also 'As easy as ABC' on page 117).

E = Evidence or Examples. Illustrate your points with tangible examples, for instance from your own experience. Use facts and figures by all means, but it is often more effective if your examples have a human dimension, so anecdotes or scenarios can be powerful.

A = Audience. Adjust the message to make it appropriate for each specific audience and the media outlet(s) in which you're appearing. Try to understand each audience's likely concerns, values and needs. Do, however, ensure a consistent message, even though the precise wording might vary for different audiences.

N = Negatives. While it's not necessarily helpful to dwell too much on negatives, it may be helpful to spend a little time thinking what the most likely negative questions might be, as these will often be quite predictable. Try asking yourself 'What's the worst question they could ask?' and rehearse your response accordingly.

Going through the I MEAN approach before an interview is a good way to prepare, to ensure you get across what *you mean* to say.

A sense of rumour

Many crisis management plans include the huge assumption that staff won't talk to the media, usually because an edict along those lines was issued in the dim and distant past. Some plans might even contain a prompt to give them a little reminder, which is all well and good.

But firstly, that edict in itself won't guarantee their silence. Secondly, the news media aren't the only communications channel to your stakeholders, even though it's the area that often gets all the focus – and paranoia. Thirdly and, perhaps, most importantly, is the fact that every one of your employees is a potential public relations representative, whether your crisis management team wants them to be or not!

You can issue edicts not to talk to the media until you're blue in the face but that won't stop your people talking to other people. Think about it – you can't tell them to stop talking to customers, suppliers or other stakeholders, particularly if their normal jobs involve that contact. And then there's the huge, wriggly can of worms that social media provides.

So rather than just telling them who they can't talk to, do you tell them who they can? Do you give them any guidance on what information they can share? Do you keep them sufficiently informed about what's going on and what messages you *want* communicated?

The trouble is, in the absence of hard information, the rumour mill will very quickly start up and fill the void. That's its job and it does it very well. But once it starts it can be very difficult to control and almost impossible to stop.

People will talk, whether you like it or not. But if you keep them informed you'll have some influence over the content of those conversations, rather than them consisting mostly of rumour and speculation.

So make sure your crisis communications plan contains, at its core, a well-thought-out rumour control strategy – which is largely about allowing people to talk, but ensuring that you provide them with something to talk about.

Follow-up actions

This page is for you to note any tips from this chapter that struck a chord, along with the follow-up actions you intend to take to benefit your business continuity management programme in your organisation.

TIP/PAGE...	TO MAKE THIS TIP WORK FOR ME I WILL...

Chapter 7

People Issues

When dealing with people, let us remember we are not dealing with creatures of logic. We are dealing with creatures of emotion...

> – Dale Carnegie, *How to Win Friends and Influence People* (1936)

Keeping one's own counsel

It may sound obvious, but disasters or major incidents affect people as well as systems, processes or facilities. Depending on the circumstances, some may be mildly concerned or upset; some may be severely traumatised; others may fall somewhere in between. But there's a fair chance that most of those involved will be affected in some way.

Many business continuity plans recognise this fact, but how many plans go further than a bullet point or two along the lines of 'contact the counselling service' buried in one of the checklists?

Frankly, this isn't good enough, and it betrays a lack of awareness about how people might actually be affected and what their needs might really be. In fact, many experts agree that counselling isn't usually appropriate at all in the first few days or even weeks. Intervention of this type too early may interfere with normal recovery processes, and so should be used with caution.

There are some very good reasons for looking after your people, from basic humanity through to ensuring they are able to return to work and be productive – notwithstanding the fact that your duty of care as an employer extends to their mental as well as their physical health. So surely they deserve a little more thought than a line that says 'contact the counselling service' in your business continuity plan?

Personal effects

Business continuity management, in its various guises, has been around for some time now. Long enough for a whole industry to have grown up around it. There are oodles of useful products and services available these days to help us ensure the continuity of our businesses. IT and telephony recovery solutions, emergency accommodation, crisis communication tools, transport, salvage and restoration services – the list goes on.

As an industry, it's fair to say that we generally do the physical infrastructure and facilities stuff pretty well now. Where we're usually not so hot, however, is on the people side.

We often spend huge amounts of time and money on implementing and testing our various technical recovery solutions, but as often as not we pay little or no attention to the human aspects of business continuity management.

For instance, we make massive assumptions about what people will be willing and able to do following some sort of disaster or major disruptive incident. Like the idea that they'll happily relocate at a moment's notice and work perfectly normally in some unfamiliar, far-flung location for weeks on end; or that working from home for as long as we need them to will be a breeze for everyone. While we might consider how to physically get them there or provide them with a laptop and an internet connection, we usually give scant consideration to the practical or personal issues or the emotional or psychological impacts that might arise.

Worse still, we seldom challenge or validate those potentially flawed assumptions, either by research or testing, or (cue sharp intake of breath!) by actually discussing them with the people concerned.

If all this sounds uncomfortably familiar, perhaps now is the time to shift the focus a little bit and start giving those 'people issues' the consideration that they deserve.

Self, self, self

As touched on in the previous tip, 'Personal effects', most business continuity plans pay scant regard to how people might be feeling in the aftermath of a major disruptive incident and simply assume their willingness and ability to drop everything in order to activate those plans.

This assumption might be valid if the incident in question is limited in scope – such as a building, facilities, IT or supply chain issue – and doesn't result in death, injury or personal hardship. But if it's wider reaching – for instance extreme weather, earthquake, flood, power failure, civil disturbance, terrorist incident, pandemic or any of a whole host of other potential events that affect the wider community – there's a major problem with it.

The fact is that people are likely to be thinking of themselves, their families and their homes, rather than the organisation they work for. In which case, the business continuity plan is likely to rank somewhere near the bottom of the list of things on their minds. And their willingness to drop everything and come to the aid of the organisation is, perfectly reasonably, likely to be somewhere between low and zero.

Most people have lives, and responsibilities, outside of work. But it's much easier to simply ignore this important fact when creating our business continuity plans, than to worry too much about it. So that's precisely what many planners do. The trouble with this approach, however, is that while our plans might look OK on paper, they could well be doomed to failure from the outset if we actually have to put them into operation.

Let's get personal

When creating our crisis/incident management or business continuity plans, it's common to think of people in terms of their roles within those plans or within the organisation. So, people tend to get pigeonholed – as the chief executive, or the crisis/incident management team leader, or the media spokesperson, or whoever.

While it's obviously important to consider the roles of these key players, it's also important to consider that, first and foremost, they are people. And people – yes, even senior people! – have lives outside of work and have their own personal issues and concerns, as well as those of the organisation.

POWER TIP

When a crisis hits, it's only natural that people don't only see themselves in their professional roles, but also see themselves as themselves – a parent; a spouse or partner; a son or daughter; a home-owner; a person who's also experiencing the stresses and strains of the crisis. Depending on the prevailing situation, these personal concerns may well be uppermost in their minds. So, in order for them to be effective in their assigned roles, they have to be allowed to address their own personal issues.

It's very easy to assume, when creating our plans, that people will prioritise their crisis/incident management or business continuity roles over their personal ones. But if we do this, things may not go as smoothly as anticipated when we try to put those plans into operation.

We're only human

'Self, self, self' on page 128 discusses the lack of consideration in most business continuity plans for people's feelings post-incident, in the context of how this, and their personal responsibilities, might make it impossible for them to drop everything and come to the aid of the organisation.

Another consideration that's just as often overlooked is that how people are feeling might impact on their ability to respond, even if they are willing and able to do so.

Because depending on the incident in question, stress, fear, panic or other emotions may well render people incapable of clear or rational thought, or of following complicated instructions. In which case, what they absolutely don't need is a 40, 50 or 60-plus-page, highly detailed plan – particularly one that they've never seen before.

In these circumstances, what people really need are simple, easy-to-follow processes and/or clear, concise instructions that don't come as a surprise, because they've been adequately briefed and trained on them in advance.

And, by the way, this applies as much to the senior people in the crisis or incident management team as it does to the more junior people 'on the ground'. Because, like it or not, we're all human and we're all subject, to varying degrees, to those feelings and emotions and their potential impacts.

It's important that we recognise these issues and address them in our planning by:

- ensuring that we have alternates or deputies to key personnel
- simplifying our plans as much as possible, perhaps substituting verbiage for checklists, flowcharts or other diagrams
- raising awareness of said plans and people's roles and responsibilities in the event that they're activated

- exercising and testing, which should include, in one form or another, everyone who's likely to be involved – which means not concentrating solely on the 'big hitters' in the crisis or incident management team
- putting in place mechanisms to follow up with people affected by an incident to help ensure their well-being.

Alternatively, we could do none of the above and just keep our fingers crossed.

One at a time

Much has been written on the subject of stress, including the difference between 'good stress', which is said to motivate us and make us perform better, and 'bad stress', which hinders rather than helps performance. The latter type can seriously affect our decision-making capability, sap our energy and, at the extreme, affect our health and well-being.

The stress associated with managing a crisis is usually well above the level of good stress and can often creep into bad stress territory.

Bad stress is often caused by feelings of overwhelm; trying to deal with too many things at once – exactly the situation that members of a crisis or incident management team can find themselves in – and failing to do any of them effectively.

There's plenty of recent research that dispels the myth of multitasking, which is really just doing one thing at a time but switching quickly between two or more activities. Conventional wisdom has it that multitasking is far less efficient than concentrating on one thing at a time, which, conveniently enough, is also one of the key ways to reduce stress.

So, if doing one thing at a time is both more efficient and reduces stress, the answer to our crisis management bad stress issue seems clear – to ensure that, wherever possible, each team member has one key thing at a time to focus on, rather than everyone getting involved with every issue, as can often be the case.

For this to happen, the team needs clearly defined and understood roles and responsibilities, discipline, a strong team leader and practice. So here's a suggestion – if your team doesn't operate like this already, why not give it a try during your next crisis management exercise?

Personnel responsibility

Many of us will, at some point, have said we've had a 'traumatic' experience, when all that really happened was that we suffered some inconvenience or perhaps got a bit stressed. And while it wasn't very pleasant, it wasn't really traumatic.

So how many of us know what trauma actually means?

One definition of trauma is 'an emotional wound or shock that creates substantial, lasting damage to a person's psychological development',[7] which is somewhat different to the day-to-day 'trauma' that most of us will have encountered.

There are a number of factors involved in the cause of trauma, including:

➤ the speed of transition from normality to the traumatic event

➤ the length and level of exposure

➤ previous personal experiences, the memories of which may be triggered by the traumatic event

➤ how people are treated afterwards.

We have little or no control over the first three, but we do potentially have a big influence over the fourth – but only if we plan and prepare properly, so that we can respond appropriately when the need arises. For instance, by designating an emergency response team to deal with people, as opposed to facilities or IT or business processes – and ensuring that they have sufficient knowledge and understanding of the effects of trauma to carry out this critical role; or by training our own staff rather than relying on a third party (who we may never have spoken to, let alone checked their qualifications, and who may not even be available when needed).

It's very easy to do the wrong things when dealing with the effects of trauma (for instance by providing inadequate counselling or by counselling too early or by ignoring the subject completely). But it's also quite easy to do the right thing – with a bit of forethought and planning.

So do think seriously about the provision you've made within your crisis/incident management or business continuity plans, and consider whether the one-liner that says something like 'refer staff to the counselling service' really is adequate.

A little knowledge can be dangerous

In this tip, we return to the subject of trauma and, more specifically, post-traumatic stress disorder, or PTSD.

Many of us are familiar with the name and the abbreviation. Some of us may even be 'armchair experts', having seen the odd TV programme or movie which touches on the subject. But few of us will understand in any depth its symptoms or its consequences.

In the context of our business continuity plans, however, it's amazing how many of us think we know how PTSD should be treated – which, incidentally, usually takes the form of providing would-be sufferers with the phone number of a third-party counselling service who we've never actually spoken to and whose capabilities, in what is after all a very specialised field, we don't have the foggiest idea of.

The first thing to point out is that PTSD isn't a sign of weakness. It's a *normal* reaction of *normal people* to an *abnormal experience*. Its symptoms include (and, by the way, the following comes courtesy of a real expert, trauma counselling trainer Rosie Heath, not from the author having watched a TV programme or read a book):

- involuntary, intrusive and distressing recollections, images or thoughts
- flashbacks, where the individual feels that the event is actually recurring
- nightmares and other sleep disturbances
- hyper-arousal, such as exaggerated startle responses, irritability or difficulty concentrating
- emotional numbing, such as feeling detached from others or inability to experience feelings.

Anyone surviving a traumatic event (whatever their level of seniority) is likely to suffer some or all of the above symptoms. This is completely normal and, in most cases, should improve over a matter of weeks or (in more extreme cases) months.

Importantly – and this is the main thing that we armchair experts often get hopelessly wrong – the real experts tend to agree that *counselling is not appropriate in the first few weeks* and may actually cause more harm than good.

They often suggest a thing called 'the watchful wait', whereby there is no psychological intervention within the first 4–6 weeks, but people are given the opportunity to talk and listen.

Should counselling be considered appropriate after that, the counsellor must be *trauma* trained if the sessions are to be helpful. This may sound blindingly obvious, but not all counsellors are and checking is something that's frequently overlooked.

So by all means include the phone number of a counselling service in your business continuity plan. But do be aware of when it is and isn't appropriate to call on them. And do at least make the effort to check out the people who may be asked to counsel your people – to find out what they can offer and to confirm that they have the appropriate skills and experience to do so. The consequences, for our people and for our businesses, are far too serious to get it wrong.

A personnel challenge?

One assumption that's very often made is that the HR department will handle any and all people issues that might arise as a result of invoking our incident management or business continuity plans. Which, on the surface, probably seem like a reasonable assumption to make. But let's just take a moment to think about what that might mean.

For a start, what do we mean by 'people issues'? This might range from looking after staff who have been asked to temporarily relocate, or determining changes to relevant policies such as travel and subsistence or working hours, through to dealing with injured or traumatised people and/or their nearest and dearest.

And therein lies the potential problem. Because many HR departments aren't actually adequately prepared to deal with the latter and have absolutely no experience of doing so. To quote one HR director, 'Our HR don't do compassion.' While that remark might sound a bit harsh and uncaring, it wasn't meant that way. The point being made was that in that particular organisation, HR need to be neutral in their business-as-usual role. And, in any case, the role of the HR department in question, like so many others, is more to do with managing the day-to-day people issues and associated processes – such as recruitment, starters and leavers, appraisals, training, payroll, personnel records and the like. All of which are about a zillion miles away from having to speak to anxious or bereaved relatives or deal with traumatised people.

So why do we assume that our HR folks will be capable of doing these things, just because they do 'people' stuff in their day jobs?

It may well be that your HR people are the obvious ones to deal with the 'people issues'. But that's only going to work if they're adequately skilled, trained, prepared and personally capable of doing what can be an extremely difficult job. Are yours?

POWER TIP

Touchy feely

The tips in this chapter discuss some of the people issues associated with business continuity management and several suggest that people deserve more consideration than they often get. They challenge the common assumption that people will be willing and able to do whatever we ask them to, whenever and wherever we want them to, no matter what's happening around them.

Some of us understand that people aren't the same as other assets; that they're complex and sensitive creatures, not machines; that they often need looking after if we're to get the best out of them and prevent them from breaking down; and that they might just have other priorities and commitments and worries outside of work.

Others will no doubt think this is all a bit 'touchy feely' and unnecessary; that people should just pull themselves together, get on with it and do as they're told. And we're all entitled to our opinions, no matter how mistaken or misguided they might be.

Whichever camp you're in, one thing's for sure – if you want to be confident that your strategies and plans will, in fact, work when you need them to, you can't just ignore the people issues and continue with those flawed assumptions.

The fact is that people will be much more likely and much more able to support the organisation's recovery efforts if their other issues and concerns are eased.

So even if it's against your nature, a bit of 'touchy feely' consideration of your people's needs and worries and personal circumstances actually makes good sense – even if your motive is simply to get your 'assets' (or, as some of us prefer to call them, *people*) up and running and working effectively again as soon as possible.

Follow-up actions

This page is for you to note any tips from this chapter that struck a chord, along with the follow-up actions you intend to take to benefit your business continuity management programme in your organisation.

TIP/PAGE...	TO MAKE THIS TIP WORK FOR ME I WILL...

Chapter 8
Exercising and Testing

Before anything else, preparation is the key to success.
  – Alexander Graham Bell

The proof of the pudding

It's all very well having a business continuity plan that looks good on paper, but it can't be relied upon until we've proved that it will work and that our assumptions are valid. So, short of staging our own crisis or disaster, that means exercising and testing. And we're unlikely to get the most from our exercises and tests unless we plan and prepare for them properly.

A properly planned and managed exercise or test will include most, if not all, of the following:

- management and coordination
- objectives and success criteria
- risk assessment
- an exercise/test plan and schedule
- briefing of participants
- event logs and post-exercise/test critique forms
- independent observers
- debriefing of participants
- post-exercise/test reporting and follow-up of actions.

The proof of the pudding may be in the eating, but the proof of the business continuity plan is in the exercising and testing. So make sure you have a recipe for success.

A successful failure?

A business continuity exercise or test can be a big deal for some organisations, often requiring significant investment in time, resources and/or money. So, not unreasonably, there's usually a desire for the exercise and test to be 'successful'. But what does 'success' mean?

For the less enlightened, successful may translate as problem free. Indeed, some may see it as a failure if an exercise or test doesn't go perfectly. But this really is rather spectacularly missing the point.

POWER TIP

While a problem-free exercise or test may be seen by some as a success, this can give a completely false sense of security. The most successful ones are, in fact, those which identify issues and potential problems, allowing improvements to be made to plans, processes and procedures, thereby increasing the likelihood of success if they ever have to be activated for real. In other words, an exercise or test that doesn't go 100% smoothly is not necessarily a 'failure'.

If we fall into the trap of going for a 'tick in the box' and make our exercises or tests too easy or, worse, engineer them so as to guarantee 'success', we may well be setting ourselves up for a fall. Surely it's far better to flush out the gremlins in the safe environment of an exercise or test than have them catch us out when it really matters.

Ready for anything?

'A bag of spanners?' on page 76 explores the pros and cons of developing scenario-based plans and suggested that they probably aren't the best approach for most organisations.

That's not to say, however, that scenarios aren't useful elsewhere in the business continuity management process. Indeed, they can be extremely beneficial in exercising and testing our plans.

A really effective way to prove our strategies and solutions, flush out the gremlins, highlight issues that we may not previously have considered, raise awareness and develop the capability of the key players is to walk through our plans and the associated activities in the context of some scenarios. All of which constitutes a pretty good reason for giving it a whirl.

And it's a good idea to test our plans against a number of different scenarios, as it's likely that different scenarios will tease out different issues. For instance, our plan might cope admirably with a fire at the head office during working hours, but will it be as effective in the event of a similar incident out of hours? or a denial of access due to a neighbour's problem? or a supply chain failure? or a loss of key staff? or an issue that attracts negative media attention?... or a combination of several of those things.

Exercising and testing our plans against a number of different scenarios will ensure they're robust, effective and flexible. Which they need to be. Because, when all's said and done, it's impossible to be sure in advance of exactly which scenario we might have to deal with.

Imagine that

'Ready for anything?' on the previous page suggests exercising and testing our business continuity strategies, solutions and plans against a number of scenarios, as it's likely that different scenarios will highlight different issues.

So here are a few examples that you might consider:

- Denial of access to your premises. This could be short, long term or indefinite and could be due to either a neighbour's problem or one of your own (examples include fire, flood, asbestos, chemical spill, industrial accident or crime).

- Computer hardware stolen or impounded under an evidence preservation order.

- Supply chain disruption, which may be the result of protest or a fuel strike or the unavailability of components or raw materials or the failure of a key supplier.

- A prolonged utility failure, such as a power or telecommunications outage, affecting just your site or a wider area.

- Negative media attention, as a result of the activities of the organisation or its employees.

- IT outage and/or significant data loss, due to hardware/software failure or cyber attack.

- Loss or unavailability of key employees or multiple employees (due to accident, illness, or even a lottery win).

The possibilities are almost endless, limited only by your imagination and the willingness of the participants to get involved.

You might draw the line at a zombie attack, which has actually been used by several organisations. Then again, you might not!

Keep fit

Many of us make New Year's resolutions each year, one of the most common of which is to exercise regularly.

Some of us may want to maintain or improve upon what is already a reasonable level of fitness. Others may want to get fit in the first place, perhaps because we've let ourselves go a bit and aren't exactly in peak condition. Some may want to become fit enough to carry out a particular activity, such as playing a sport.

But it's not just our own personal physical fitness that will benefit from regular exercising. Our business continuity 'fitness' can be significantly improved in a similar way.

Fitter usually means more able to carry out the activity that we're training and exercising for. In a business continuity context, 'fitter' means more capable of carrying out our assigned roles, whether they're associated with incident or crisis management, infrastructure recovery or business recovery.

Fitter usually means leaner and more agile. In a business continuity context, the 'fitter' and more capable our teams are, the leaner our incident management and recovery plans can potentially be.

Then there's the important matter of fitness for purpose. In a business continuity context that applies to our strategies, solutions and plans. If we never exercise them we'll never know for sure whether they're up to the job.

So why not resolve to implement a business continuity exercise programme as well as a personal one? And, just as importantly, to stick to this resolution for more than a couple of weeks!

Warts and all

Whether we're conducting a scenario-based crisis management or business recovery exercise, an IT or user relocation test or some other type of rehearsal, there's often a fair bit at stake for those involved in the event.

For instance, there may well be a significant amount of management and staff time invested in preparing and carrying out the exercise; the planners and facilitators may feel that their ability or reputation is on the line; the IT department may feel that their technical capability is under the spotlight; or the person responsible for implementing the continuity strategy may feel that their credibility is at stake.

Whatever the reason, when the exercise or test is over and we're writing the report, it can be tempting to focus almost entirely on the positives and gloss over the negatives. In fact some test reports take this to the extreme and end up as nothing more than a back-slapping exercise. But if we don't tell the whole story we're missing a trick.

Of course it's important to recognise the successes and to give credit where it's due, but in doing so there's a danger that the stuff that didn't go so well doesn't get sufficient attention. The result is that problems aren't fixed or issues aren't resolved, which is one of the main reasons for carrying out the exercise or test in the first place. In order to avoid this, the post-exercise report needs to be honest and tell it as it was – warts and all.

We shouldn't be afraid to include comments on what didn't go so well or to point out what hasn't yet been tested – and therefore what risks remain. In doing so the report doesn't have to suggest that the test or exercise was a failure (indeed, a test or exercise that highlights problems or issues should be seen as a success rather than a failure) but it should recognise the work that still needs to be done.

So don't be afraid to tell it like it is, good and bad. Indulge in a bit of mutual back-slapping by all means, but don't completely bury the bad news – it may just come back to haunt you if you do.

Are you sitting comfortably?

For many organisations, a crisis management or business continuity exercise is seen as a necessary evil, conducted grudgingly every year or two in order to address an audit finding or tick a compliance box. Because of this, and/or the ever-popular justification that 'some of the team members have changed since the last exercise, and we don't want to put the new ones under too much pressure', the resulting exercise is often far from challenging, comprising a fairly low-key discussion of the issues that might arise, rather than any kind of realistic, stretching event.

A discussion-based approach is all well and good for a first exercise – after all there is much value in identifying issues and follow-up actions in this way – but this 'comfortable' type of exercise doesn't usually challenge the participants to any great extent and certainly doesn't adequately prepare them for the real thing.

We'd probably all agree that our respective fire services are pretty good at putting out fires. This is largely because, when they're not putting out 'real' fires, they practise putting out fires. And the fires that they practise on, although not real in the sense that it's not someone's home or office that's ablaze, are actual fires, with real flames and smoke and real actions taken to deal with their effects. A key point here is that the firefighters typically don't just sit around a table, enjoying coffee and biscuits, and have a nice cosy chat about how they might put out a theoretical fire or carry a theoretical person down a theoretical ladder; they physically go through the actual processes involved.

That's not to say that the cosy chat approach isn't beneficial from an educational point of view, particularly for new recruits, but it's usually the precursor to involvement in a series of far more realistic exercises.

While it's not being suggested here that we should actually torch our building for the purposes of an exercise, there are many ways in which we can make our exercises more realistic and challenging. And, rather than treating each exercise as a one-off, box-ticking activity, making it deliberately low key so it's not too difficult for the new players, we should think in terms of a programme of exercises, raising the bar each time. If we're really worried about how any new team members might cope, we should seriously consider a separate, initial cosy chat-type session before the main event, rather than keeping the bar low for everyone.

Testing the limits

It's generally accepted that the various types of business continuity exercises and tests typically carried out – whether scenario-based incident management exercises, IT recovery, relocation or call cascade tests – are all good things to do. And that's almost certainly true.

As often as not, however, an organisation's exercising and testing programme is designed around the types of exercise or test that are deemed practicable or achievable, with little or no consideration of the extent to which these exercises and tests contribute to proving the business continuity strategy.

Worse still, some programmes revolve around the things that are easy to do and shy away from the difficult stuff, which at best can give a false sense of security and at worst completely misses the point. For instance:

➤ conducting scenario-based exercises with the same few people every time doesn't prove that the alternates know how to put the incident management strategies into operation, or have the capability to do so.

➤ asking a few people to log on from home occasionally and check that they can access a couple of IT systems doesn't prove the strategy that says a significant proportion of a department or team will work from home for a significant period.

➤ taking several days to recover a selection of IT systems and image a few desktop PCs, followed by a member of the IT team logging on to check that systems can be accessed, doesn't prove the strategy that says dozens or hundreds of people will relocate to and conduct business from the recovery site for a prolonged period.

➤ telling people that a call cascade test will be carried out on a certain date (or during a certain period) doesn't prove that you'll be able to contact large numbers of people out of hours with no notice.

All of the above can give you a warm and fuzzy, though possibly spurious, feeling that everything is OK. Until, of course, you try to put your strategies into operation for real, which isn't the best time to discover that you've been deluding yourself.

POWER TIP

The best exercising and testing programmes are designed with the primary objective of proving that the business continuity strategies actually work.

Yours may be one of these, in which case a pat on the back is in order. But if it's not, you might like to give it some further consideration.

Practice makes permanent

Most people are familiar with the phrase 'practice makes perfect'.

Practice (which in a business continuity context largely means exercising, rehearsing or testing) embeds activities and eventually, through repeated practice, makes them second nature. With sufficient practice we can reach a point where, in response to the appropriate trigger, we'll automatically carry out the activity, exactly as we learned it, without having to think too much about it.

Imagine a golfer who spends hours on the driving range practising his tee shots, so that when he gets out on the course he can execute the shot consistently, without having to think about every aspect of it. So far so good.

However, the phrase 'practice makes perfect' is misleading. Because it isn't strictly true.

Practice doesn't necessarily make perfect – what it does make is *permanent*. Which means that if we practise the wrong things they can also become embedded. The result is the same in one respect – we become able to consistently carry out the activity without thinking about it. The trouble is that we can consistently do it wrong!

Back to our golfer. Now imagine that he isn't actually very good and has a tendency to slice his drives (the bane of many a high handicapper). Unless he takes some professional advice to correct the problem, the only thing that all of that practice is likely to achieve is the ability to consistently slice the ball, time after time. Not exactly the desired result!

So make sure you practise regularly, but do make sure you practise the right things. Because if people are rehearsing the wrong responses or embedding incorrect assumptions, that practice might actually be doing more harm than good.

All in good time?

These days, most organisations that 'do' business continuity understand the importance of exercising and testing. Many have comprehensive exercising and testing programmes, which include crisis/incident management exercises, IT recovery tests and user relocation tests, among others.

It's not unusual for IT recovery testing to be done out of hours, in order to minimise any risk or impact to the business. The same is sometimes true of user relocation testing. But crisis or incident management exercises are almost always conducted during office hours.

The main reason is that exercising during office hours is more convenient, both for the participants and the facilitators, and there's usually (although not always) more chance of getting the key players to attend.

But exercising during the working day also has some distinct disadvantages. It doesn't, for instance, simulate in any meaningful way a situation where those key players have to deal with a major issue when they're already tired after a busy day's work. It doesn't test out-of-hours access to facilities or people. And out of hours is precisely when small incidents have a nasty habit of turning into bigger incidents, usually exacerbated by the fact that the right people aren't around to nip them in the bud.

Organisations with a mature crisis/incident management exercising programme should give serious consideration to carrying out the occasional out-of-hours exercise. This may be a little unpopular at first, until participants get the point, so rather than going the whole hog and starting your next exercise at 2am on a Sunday, perhaps a 7pm start on a weekday would be slightly more palatable.

There may be some moans and groans at first, but these are likely to be far outweighed by the resulting improvements to your crisis/incident management capability.

An exercise is an exercise is an exercise – isn't it?

Many organisations exercise their crisis/incident management and business continuity teams and their associated plans by conducting scenario-based exercises. Which is a very good thing to do. Scenario-based exercises can help to clarify roles and responsibilities, provide a means of rehearsing activities, exercise participants, challenge and validate assumptions and test processes and plans, among other things. In short, they help to develop the participants' capability. What's more, they help to tick a box for an auditor or regulator.

But not all exercises are the same. In fact, there are many ways to conduct a scenario-based exercise. At one end of the scale there's the humble tabletop exercise, which is usually fairly low key and generally involves a discussion of the issues and associated activities that might arise. At the other end there's the all-singing, all-dancing, highly realistic, high-pressure, full-on roleplay, with actors and journalists and news reports and goodness knows what else. And between the two extremes there's a raft of facilitation methods to suit all tastes and budgets.

All of them have value, if they're if done effectively and at the appropriate times vis-à-vis the maturity of the business continuity programme and the team(s) involved.

POWER TIP

But let's not kid ourselves that sitting around a table having a nice cosy chat about the issues is going to fully prepare the crisis or incident management team in the way that a full-blown rehearsal will. And let's not kid ourselves that conducting an exercise (whichever end of the spectrum it falls on), that lasts an hour or two, once every couple of years, and which half of the team members are unable to attend, is going to hone the teams' capability to razor sharpness.

If all we want is a tick in a box, then a nice easy exercise every now and then will probably achieve that. But a tick in a box is not the same as a *capability*. If it's a capability that we're after, we need to develop an ongoing programme that a) involves all of the key players and b) raises the bar with each subsequent exercise.

To misquote George Orwell, 'all exercises are equal – but some are more equal than others'.

A pair of debriefs

It's fairly standard practice to hold some form of debrief at the end of an exercise or test (or, indeed, an actual incident), which is a very sensible thing to do. It helps to ensure that any issues and actions arising are captured and it's a good way to obtain feedback from the participants on how they thought things went. But some debriefs are a bit on the, well, brief side.

Because it comes at the end of what can sometimes be a lengthy or challenging, sometimes stressful, session, it can be all too easy to make the debrief too brief. There can be a temptation to let people 'get away' so that they can return to their day jobs. But the danger is that, once they do so, all the good stuff that the exercise teased out will be forgotten within a couple of weeks or, at best, vaguely remembered but not given the attention it deserves.

That's not to suggest that the debrief should be overly lengthy, just that sufficient time should be allowed to ensure that everything that needs to be captured is, so that a follow-up action plan can be agreed.

And, while it may seem like a bit of a luxury, it can be very beneficial to hold two debriefs – a 'hot' debrief immediately after the exercise or test and a second, 'cold' debrief a couple of weeks later, after the dust has settled.

Go on, be honest, how brief are your debriefs? And how many do you do? If you don't already do so, why not give the double-debrief a try after your next exercise or test and see what the results are like?

Follow-up actions

This page is for you to note any tips from this chapter that struck a chord, along with the follow-up actions you intend to take to benefit your business continuity management programme in your organisation.

TIP/PAGE...	TO MAKE THIS TIP WORK FOR ME I WILL...

One final tip

Assuming you've made it this far, you've probably ploughed your way through most, if not all, of the preceding 101 tips.

Not all of them will necessarily apply to, or be implementable in, your organisation, but a number of them almost certainly will. You may even have made a few notes on the 'Follow-up actions' pages at the end of each chapter – that is, after all, what they were put there for.

You now have a choice...

You could simply put this book on your bookshelf with your other business continuity books – perhaps next to the original *Practical Business Continuity Management* if you have a copy of that one too (if not, it's still available at www.acumen-bcp.co.uk). Alternatively, you could pass it on to someone else – although the author would much rather you recommended it to them instead, so that they buy their own copy!

Or you could have a go at putting some of the tips into practice. You now have, after all, a plethora of good ideas and pieces of sound advice, at least some of which could benefit the business continuity management programme in your organisation.

So why not resolve to implement at least one of those good ideas? Perhaps the one that made you think 'hmm, that might just work here' when you read it? And why not do it sooner, rather than later? After all, there's no time like the present.

And if it does work, don't forget there are another 100 tips that you could try!

Thanks for reading and all the best to you and your business continuity management programme.

Endnotes

[1] ISO 22301 Societal Security – Preparedness and continuity management systems – Requirements (International Organization for Standardization).

[2] AS/NZS 5050:2010 Business continuity – Managing disruption-related risk (Standards Australia).

[3] NFPA 1600 Standard on Continuity, Emergency, and Crisis Management (US National Fire Protection Association).

[4] 'What if?' and 'So what?' are two questions that can help with crisis management decision-making. In other words, what might be the consequences of a particular decision or if a particular event occurs? And are the consequences acceptable? Originally described in *Practical Business Continuity Management* (section entitled 'Questions, questions').

[5] The 'CARE' message and its use are described in more detail in *Practical Business Continuity Management* (section entitled 'Take CARE').

[6] Cyril Northcote Parkinson was a British naval historian and author of some 60 books, including *Parkinson's Law, or The Pursuit of Progress*, which includes the adage that 'work expands so as to fill the time available for its completion'.

[7] Alexander, J., Eyerman, R., et al. *Cultural trauma and collective identity*, 2004.

References

'The magnificent seven' was prompted by the article 'Rule of 7: The Ideal Work Group Size' by Sean Silverthorne, which in turn referenced the book *Decide & Deliver: 5 Steps to Breakthrough Performance in Your Organization* by Marcia W. Blenko, Michael C. Mankins, and Paul Rogers as the source of the statement that each additional member (over seven) reduces decision effectiveness by 10%.

The idea behind 'The deciding factor' came from the article 'Decision fatigue in crisis management: modern day challenges of multi-tasking incident managers' by Paul Kudray.

'Log it or lose it' was inspired by a presentation on the importance of event and decision logging by solicitor advocate Mark Scoggins.

The original ideas for 'In search of the TRUTH' and 'As easy as ABC' came from the book *Handling the Media* by Magnus Carter.

'Making a statement' is based on a 'Quickfire Media Training Tip' by Dave Mason of Mentor Training.

The original idea for 'I MEAN to say' came from Dave Mason's book *Handling the Media in Good Times & Bad*.

'Personnel Responsibility' and 'A little knowledge can be dangerous' are based on concepts and advice developed by Rosie Heath.

Acknowledgements

I would like to thank the following people, all experienced business and/or IT continuity professionals and practitioners, who kindly took the time to review and comment on various drafts of the manuscript:

Kevin Bennett, former consultant and business continuity manager (retired)

Sarah Cotterill, global head of business continuity management, Computacenter

Daman Dev Sood, COO, Continuity & Resilience

Rob Fletcher, head of ICT, GreenSquare Group

David Honour, managing editor, Continuity Central

Mark Mahoney, business continuity professional

Nigel Mortimer, consultant, Trustmarque

Rob Osborn, business continuity consultant, Osborn BC

Need some help?

We all need a bit of help or guidance now and again. Whether we're new to business continuity management and want to benefit from the experience of someone who's 'been there and done it', or experienced practitioners who can benefit from a fresh pair of eyes or a different approach.

Andy Osborne provides the following business continuity consultancy services to clients, through his company, Acumen:

➤ Business continuity health check/capability review

➤ Business impact analysis

➤ Risk assessment

➤ Dependency modelling

➤ Emergency response and crisis/incident management planning

➤ Business continuity strategy and plan development

➤ Exercising and testing

➤ Training and awareness, including the following courses:

 – Business continuity management fundamentals

 – Crisis/incident management fundamentals

 – Risk management fundamentals

 – Human aspects of business continuity/incident management

 – Exercising and testing

 – Media interview skills and crisis media management

 – Social media crisis management

 – Bespoke training courses, workshops, briefing/awareness sessions and scenario-based exercises

- Crisis communications preparedness (including media training)
- Mobile app-based incident response/management plans
- Ad hoc advice and guidance

To contact Andy, call +44 (0)1386 834455 or email him at aosborne@acumen-bcp.co.uk.

Tip of the Month

If you've found the tips in this book useful, why not subscribe to Andy Osborne's Tip of the Month and have additional tips emailed to you each month.

To subscribe, either complete the registration form on the Acumen website (www.acumen-bcp.co.uk) or email Andy at aosborne@acumen-bcp.co.uk.

Printed in Great Britain
by Amazon